KT-140-159

CityPack
Madrid

JONATHAN HOLLAND

Jonathan Holland was born in 1961. He moved to Madrid in 1990, having lived for five years in southern Italy. As well as being a fiction writer (his novel The Escape Artist *was published in 1994), he teaches literature at Madrid's Complutense University and is a regular contributor of articles to various magazines.*

City-centre map continues on inside back cover

AA Publishing

Contents

About this book 4

best 49–60

where to ... 61–86

travel facts 87–93

About this book

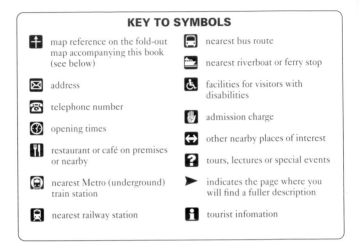

KEY TO SYMBOLS

✚ map reference on the fold-out map accompanying this book (see below)

✉ address

☎ telephone number

🕐 opening times

🍴 restaurant or café on premises or nearby

Ⓜ nearest Metro (underground) train station

🚉 nearest railway station

🚌 nearest bus route

⛴ nearest riverboat or ferry stop

♿ facilities for visitors with disabilities

✋ admission charge

↔ other nearby places of interest

❓ tours, lectures or special events

➤ indicates the page where you will find a fuller description

ℹ tourist infomation

CityPack Madrid is divided into six sections to cover the six most important aspects of your visit to Madrid. It includes:

- An introduction to the city and its people
- Itineraries, walks and excursions
- The top 25 sights to visit
- Features about different aspects of the city that make it special
- Detailed listings of restaurants, hotels, shops and nightlife
- Practical information

In addition, easy-to-read side panels provide fascinating extra facts and snippets, highlights of places to visit and invaluable practical advice.

CROSS-REFERENCES

To help you make the most of your visit, cross-references, indicated by ➤, show you where to find additional information about a place or subject.

MAPS

- **The fold-out map** in the wallet at the back of the book is a comprehensive street plan of Madrid. All the map references given in the book refer to this map. For example, the Museo Cerralbo at Calle Ventura Rodríguez 17 has the following information: ✚ C8 indicating the grid square of the map in which the Museo Cerralbo will be found.
- **The city-centre maps** found on the inside front and back covers of the book itself are for quick reference. They show the top 25 sights, described on pages 24–48, which are clearly plotted by number (**1** – **25**, not page number) from west to east across the city.

MADRID
life

INTRODUCING MADRID

The *siesta*

Despite pronounced efforts at modernisation, old traditions die hard in Madrid. The *siesta*, an anomalously old-fashioned habit in a city trying so hard to be modern, looks stubbornly healthy – for a while anyway. You may be frustrated at finding so many shops and museums closed for two hours or more at lunchtime. To enjoy Madrid to the full, it is best to try to adapt to how the locals live. The *siesta* is, after all, a testament to the *madrileños* vivacity: at 1 AM on a weekday morning, any central bar will still be full of people of all ages chatting away. People eat late and go to bed late; dinner is often not taken before 10 or 11 at night, even in winter; in summer the 'night' is still young at 3.30 AM. Yet, in recent years even the *siesta* has become threatened, as business practices try to come in line with the rest of northern Europe. One result of this is that *madrileños* are functioning on less and less sleep, a fact generating great interest– and worry – to Spanish health watchdogs.

Beyond clichés like 'wonderfully chaotic', 'energetic', 'magisterial', and 'from Madrid to Heaven', it's a challenge to define Madrid. At the north end of the city, skyscrapers rise and hi-tech buildings bustle with men and women working to fulfil Prime Minister José Maria Aznar's promise to make Madrid a world power in the new millennium. In the south, a world away from the hotels, restaurants and museums, abject poverty reigns: shanty towns where wood is burned for warmth and where there is no concrete, only mud. To the west lies the Casa de Campo, a huge expanse of sometimes beautiful, sometimes brutal greenery around which the city has had to mould itself; and above is the arching sky, fiercely blue and seeming so close you could touch it.

Madrileños see the city in terms of their *barrio*, or neighbourhood, and because the city is mostly made up of people whose families immigrated from other areas of Spain they tend to enthuse about the *pueblo* their family comes from rather than the city as a whole. Each *barrio* has a clearly defined profile: leafy avenues and showy wealth characterise the *barrio Salamanca*, glassy skyscrapers the AZCA district, and homely sounds and smells the labyrinthine *barrio popular*, that small triangle just south of Sol that is a melting-pot of different nationalities. Here picturesque things happen on every corner, and you are continually reminded how far Madrid has come in taking its place alongside the rest of Europe.

History books tell of medieval, Habsburg and Bourbon Madrid: a city that unlike most European capital cities did not evolve as the nation's capital, but was chosen by Philip II in 1561, as much for its position in the centre of Spain as for political reasons few historians have been able to explain. Following this, it developed rapidly with consecutive monarchs transforming the city during the next 400 years. Still within living memory of many is Madrid's heroic resistance at the end of the Civil War, and much

Puerta del Sol, at the
heart of the city

of the civic pride seen today in *madrileños* descends from the jaunty confidence that led to the anti-fascist clashes in the city during the oppressive Franco years. The cultural regeneration of the 1980s provoked by the death of General Franco and symbolised by the film director Pedro Almodóvar known as the *movida* has today modernised and greatly altered Madrid, making it a city of both great wealth and gruelling poverty. Madrid runs the gamut from high unemployment to booming industrialisation, and nowhere feels like the hub and centre of the city. Often the focus of the city's economic problems, young *madrileños* are also the movers and shakers of its exuberant social life; its image-consciousness and obsessive nocturnal *joie de vivre*. The young, whose aspirations and enterprise – or the lack of them – have embraced the values and ideals of the new millennium with breezy enthusiasm, widening the gap between generations. To them there is no doubt that Madrid's nightlife is best in Europe. The elderly know Madrid as a city that has changed beyond belief in the last quarter of a century – a city that is rapidly becoming economically, politically and technologically an important part of Europe.

Madrid is difficult for outsiders to grasp. Its spirit is elusive and diffused and will repeatedly surprise you. Most *madrileños* are used to receiving visitors. Barmen who a few years ago would

A good base for excursions

Madrid is divided into 21 *barrios*. Logically, the most central part of the city is the *centro* district. The *centro* area south of the Puerta del Sol is known as the *barrio popular*, or 'people's quarter', and is a picturesque maze of winding streets. Further south are the poorer *barrios* of Arganzuela and Moratalaz, which are the result of Madrid's expansion since the 1950s – to sample life off the tourist trail. West from Sol are the Plaza Mayor and the Royal Palace. To the east of the Paseo del Prado, the Paseo de Recoletos and the Paseo de la Castellana is the 19th-century *barrio Salamanca*. It is here, and in the Retiro and Chamberí *barrios*, south and northwest respectively, that the wealthier *madrileños* make their homes.

A passion for football

Football is a Madrid passion,and the Spanish football league – the league of stars – is home to many of the game's living legends. The Santiago Bernabeu Football Stadium, northeast of Plaza de Lima on Paseo de la Castellana, is the home of Real Madrid, historically the most successful of Madrid's teams. The football stadium holds over 90,000 spectators and is regularly used for cup finals and international games. For atmosphere, though, the Vicente Calderón – home of Madrid's second team, Atlético – is the better bet.

have screwed up their eyes in puzzlement at a foreign accent, now utter a few syllables in English. There is what is known as the *picaresca*, the epitome of the Spanish fondness for roguish wit and humour, where the *madrileños* try to see how far they can push things and get away with it, especially when it comes to making a few extra pesetas from foreign visitors. They see nothing wrong in doing this, becasuse they believe you'd do the same in their position. *Todo es negociable*, the saying goes – 'everything's negotiable' – the bargaining spirit is strong.

Getting around the city is slow due to the abundant roadworks; Madrid seems permanently under construction. Double-parking is the norm, and you can buy car-stickers that say 'Toot your horn: I'm somewhere close'. The city centre is small, and can easily be covered on foot – but pedestrian traffic can be heavy on the pavements and in tourist areas begging is rife. You are never far from other people; visitors from less demonstrative cultures are sometimes surprised by how much time *madrileños* can spend talking about absolutely nothing – and how loudly. But there is something truly life-affirming about it too. Their thoughts are trained on the outside world rather than the inner, and to every *madrileño*, another human being is always potentially an extension of the family. But with everybody out at the same time, places can get noisy and very full, forcing a large number of *madrileños* to escape to the country at weekends.

One of the perks of life in a big city

MADRID IN FIGURES

Geography
- Height of city above sea level: 655m
- Average height of Autonomous Region of Madrid: 909m
- Highest point of Autonomous Region of Madrid: 2,430m
- Surface area: 605.8sq km
- Length of Manzanares River: 86km

Population
- 929: 2,500
- 1202: 3,000
- 1440: 5,000
- 1520: 10,000
- 1561: 17,000
- 1872: 334,000
- 1920: 1,000,000
- 1960: 2,500,000
- 1998: 5,000,000

Transport
- Number of registered vehicles: 2,000,000
- Total length of Madrid road system: 3,000km
- Total length of metro system: 120km
- Number of underground lines: 10

Percentages
- Population less than 14 years old: 19 per cent
- Population more than 64 years old: 13 per cent
- Proportion of total Spanish population living in Madrid in 1860: 3 per cent
- Proportion of total Spanish population living in Madrid in 1996: 13 per cent

Firsts
- First gas lighting: 1847
- First railway line (Madrid–Aranjuez): 1851
- First film projection: 1896
- First telephone: 1880s
- First metro (Sol–Cuatro Caminos): 1919
- First cinema with sound: 1933

A CHRONOLOGY

c 1000 BC	Madrid is inhabited by Iberian tribes.
218 BC–5th century AD	Iberian peninsula under Roman rule; Madrid becomes a stopping place.
AD 711	Muslims defeat Visigoths; areas of Spain under Muslim rule for 800 years.
AD 722	Reconquest begins: Madrid becomes a strategic point of defence for Toledo.
AD 854	Muhammad I of Córdoba founds the city of Madrid.
1085	Madrid recaptured by Alfonso VI: Christians, Jews and Muslims inhabit city.
1202	Alfonso VIII recognises Madrid as a city by endowing it with Royal Statutes.
1301	Cortes, or Parliament, meets for the first time in Madrid.
15th century	Madrid becomes permanent residence of royalty.
1469	Marriage of Catholic monarchs Ferdinand and Isabella unites Aragon and Castile.
1492	Conquest of Granada; discovery of America; expulsion of the Jews; Spain begins 200-year period of imperial power.
1547	Birth of Cervantes.
1561	Philip II (1556–98) establishes Court in Madrid: cultural "Golden Age" begins.
1598	Philip III (1598–1621) first monarch to be born in Madrid.
1605	Cervantes publishes *Don Quixote*.
1617–19	Plaza Mayor built.
1665	Charles II comes to throne, aged four.

1700	Charles II dies without an heir. Philip V (1700–46) reigns as first Bourbon monarch.
1759	Charles III begins modernisation programe of Madrid.
1808–1812	French occupation; Spanish rule is restored by 1814.
1812	30,000 die from famine.
1819	Prado Museum opened, houses numbered, streets named.
1851	Madrid–Aranjuez railway line inaugurated.
1868	Revolution overthrows Isabella II.
1873	Republic declared.
1917	General strike throughout Spain.
1919	First metro line.
1931	Second Republic declared.
1936–9	Spanish Civil War, sparked by uprising in North Africa.
1975	General Francisco Franco dies. King Juan Carlos is declared his successor.
1977	First democratic General Election.
1980s	*Movida* Madrid.
1982	Socialist government elected.
1986	Spain joins the European Economic Community.
1992	Madrid is designated European Capital of Culture.
1996	Right-wing People's Party win general election, ending 14 years of socialist rule.

PEOPLE & EVENTS FROM HISTORY

Cervantes, something of a romantic hero himself

Metro stations and the famous

Many of Madrid's streets and metro stations are named after historical figures who are completely unknown outside Spain. Among the central stations, there are Tirso de Molina and Quevedo (both Golden Age writers), La Latina (the nickname of Beatriz Galindo, Queen Isabella II's Latin teacher), Rubén Darío (19th-century Nicaraguan poet), Diego de Léon (army general executed for trying to kidnap Isabella II in 1841) and Chueca (Federico Chueca, a composer of *zarzuelas*, or operettas). Most curious of all is Antón Martín, a 16th-century Valencian coastguard who converted to Christianity after seeing a vision of John the Baptist and subsequently founded the hospital in Madrid where the Reina Sofía Museum now stands. Better known are Colón (Christopher Columbus), Goya and Velázquez.

CHARLES III

Charles III, the second Bourbon king of Spain, came to the throne in 1759. A keen proponent of Enlightenment ideals, he is often known as 'the best mayor that Madrid ever had'. More than any other single historical figure, he is responsible for today's Madrid.

MIGUEL DE CERVANTES SAAVEDRA (CERVANTES)

Believed by some to be the first novel and by others simply the greatest book ever written, *Don Quixote* was published in two parts in 1605 and 1615. It's author, Cervantes, was born in Alcalá de Henares, and fought in the Battle of Lepanto (1571). Later he became a tax collector, but was imprisoned for manipulating accounts while he wrote *Don Quixote*. He died in Madrid in 1616.

GOYA

Francisco de Goya y Lucientes (1746–1848) is the painter most readily associated with Madrid, though he was neither born nor died here. Born in Aragón, he settled in Madrid in 1774 and worked at the Royal Tapestry Factory. In 1789 he became Court painter to Charles IV. In 1792, Goya contracted an illness which left him practically deaf, and it is to the silence and solitude of his convalesence that we owe the sometimes nightmarish visions of his *Caprichos (*Caprices), a series of satirical engravings. In 1814 he bought a house, the Quinta del Sordo (House of the Deaf Man), and covered the walls with the 'dark paintings' now on display in the Prado Museum.

JUAN GRIS

Painter Juan Gris (José Victoriano González), one of the great Madrid artistic exiles, was born in 1887 at Calle Tetuán 20. He began his artistic life as a cartoonist. From 1910 he dedicated himself exclusively to painting, and between 1910 and 1914 produced many of the works which make him the greatest exponent of Cubism after Picasso. He died in 1927.

MADRID
how to organise your time

13

ITINERARIES

Madrid is not forbiddingly large, though to keep a sense of historical perspective it's a good idea to concentrate on one area at a time.

ITINERARY ONE	MEDIEVAL TO HABSBURG MADRID
Morning	Plaza Mayor (➤ 33). Medieval Madrid (➤ 18). Plaza de la Villa (➤ 32). San Pedro el Viejo (➤ 55). San Andrés (➤ 54). Plaza de la Paja (➤ 53). Plaza de la Villa (➤ 32).
Lunch	Return to the Plaza Mayor to eat at Hogar Gallego (➤ 66).
Afternoon	Monasterio de la Encarnación (➤ 31). Convento de las Descalzas Reales (➤ 34).
Early evening	Return to the Plaza Major for an early evening 'apertivo' (pre-dinner drink) and then a meal at Los Galayos (➤ 64).
ITINERARY TWO	BOURBON MADRID
Morning	Plaza de Santa Ana (➤ 53). Museo del Prado (➤ 41). Casón del Buen Retiro (➤ 50). San Jerónimo el Real (➤ 42). Plaza de la Lealtad (➤ 53).
Lunch	Viridiana (➤ 62) or in the café of the Prado (➤ 41), entry from inside the museum. Good range of dishes at reasonable prices.
Afternoon	Colección Thyssen-Bornemisza (➤ 37) or Reina Sofía (➤ 38). Parque del Retiro (➤ 46). Puerta de Alcalá (➤ 45). Plaza de la Cibeles (➤ 40). Fuente de Neptuno (➤ 56).
Early evening	Drink at one of the *terraza* bars on the 'Costa Castellana' (➤ 79) and indulge in some people-watching.

ITINERARY THREE	**NORTHWESTERN MADRID**
Morning	Muralla Arabe (➤ 60). Jardines de las Vistillas (➤ 57). Catedral Nuestra Señora de la Almudena (➤ 28). Palacio Real (➤ 29).
Lunch	Café de Oriente (➤ 64). Lunch in style opposite the Royal Palace.
Afternoon	Museo Cerralbo (➤ 27). Plaza de España (➤ 52). Ermita de San Antonio (➤ 24). Stroll through Parque del Oeste (➤ 25) via La Rosaleda (➤ 25) to the *teleférico* (➤ 57). Casa de Campo (➤ 57), and then back via the *teleférico* to the Parque del Oeste.
Early evening	Templo de Debod (➤ 25), and a drink at one of the *terraza* bars on the Paseo de Pintor Rosales (➤ 79).
ITINERARY FOUR	**NORTHEAST FROM SOL**
Morning	Calle de Arenal (➤ 59). Puerta del Sol (➤ 35). Real Acadèmia de Bellas Artes de San Fernando, Calcografía Nacional (➤ 36). Jardines del Descubrimiento (➤ 44). Palacio de Bibliotecas y Museos (➤ 43). Shop in Calle de Serrano (➤ 70) and Calle José Ortega y Gasset (➤ 70).
Lunch	Teatriz (➤ 82).
Afternoon	Metro to Rubén Darío. Museo Sorolla (➤ 39), then Museo Lázaro Galdiano (➤ 47).
Early evening	Stroll round Madrid's exclusive shopping area, including Calle de Serrano and Calle Jorge Juan.

Window shopping in Calle de Serrano

15

WALKS

INFORMATION

Distance 6km
Time 3–4 hours
Start point Puerta del Sol
🚇 cII; D9
🚊 Sol (lines 1, 2, 3)
🚌 3, 5, 15, 20, 51, 52, 150 and others
End point Puerta del Sol

EAST FROM SOL

Start in the Puerta del Sol. Exit at its eastern end and walk down Calle San Jerónimo, through the Plaza de las Cortes, as far as the Neptune fountain in the Plaza de Canovas de Castillo. Turn right down the Paseo del Prado, cross it half-way down, and visit the Jardín Botánico (Botanical Gardens). Cross the plaza and walk up Calle de Felipe IV past the Royal Language Academy on your left, and the Casón del Buen Retiro. Cross Calle de Alfonso XII and enter the Retiro Park through the Felipe IV gate, and walk through the parterre gardens. Go up the steps at the end of the gardens. When you reach the lake, turn left and follow along the edge, with the Alfonso XII statue opposite you.

Exit the park at the Puerta de Alcalá and walk up Calle Serrano past the Museo Arqueológico Nacional (Archaeological Museum). Cut through the Jardines del Descubrimiento and then turn left down the Paseo de Recoletos, which runs parallel to Serrano. When you reach Barbara de Braganza, turn left and walk up past the Plaza de las Salesas. A little way past the church on the right is Calle del Barquillo, an intriguing backstreet shopping area. Go all the way down until you come to the Calle de Alcalá. Turn right and, keeping to your right, walk along the Gran Vía as far as the metro station. Then turn left down Calle de Montera and you are back in Sol.

WEST FROM SOL

Start in the Puerta del Sol. Leave it at the western end and walk up Calle de Postas to Plaza Mayor. Cross the plaza and leave it at the diagonally opposite corner (El Arco de los Cuchilleros). At the bottom of the steps cross the street and go down Calle del Maestro de la Villa into the Plaza Conde de Barajas. Explore the streets in this area, and come up into the Plaza de la Villa.

Cross Calle Mayor and walk down as far as Calle San Nicolás. Go up it, past the church and into the Plaza Ramales. Continue down the side of the Plaza de Oriente to Calle Bailén, pausing for

Opposite: the Royal Palace, from Campo del Moro

coffee at the Café del Oriente (➤ 68). Turn right and walk along the palace front. When you reach Calle San Quintin, there is a possible detour up to the Monasterio de la Encarnación.

With Plaza de Espana on your right, take the walkway under Calle Bailén, then walk up the steps to Templo de Debod, with its views of the Casa de Campo, the Royal Palace and the Almudena Cathedral. Descend the slope at the far end of Templo de Debod and cross the car park, from which a path goes down through the Parque del Oeste to the Rosaleda. When you get to Paseo del Rey, turn left and follow it as far as Cuesta de San Vicente. Go down to the Puerta de San Vicente and turn left into the Paseo de la Virgin del Puerto. On the left, about 150m down, you will find the entrance to the Campo del Moro, with the best views of the Royal Palace.

On exiting the park, continue along the Paseo de la Virgin del Puerto until you come to Calle Segovia, with the Segovia Bridge on the right. Follow Calle Segovia through the park until you come to the Arab Wall. Turn left off Calle Segovia up Costanilla de San Andrés, which will take you past the church and into Plaza de la Cebada, where there is a pleasant bar (El Viajero) at No. 11. Turn left down Calle Toledo. This leads back to Plaza Mayor and to Sol.

THE SIGHTS

- Puerta del Sol (➤ 35)
- Plaza Mayor (➤ 33)
- Plaza de la Ville (➤ 32)
- San Nicolás de los Servitas (➤ 55)
- Plaza de Oriente (➤ 30)
- Monasterio de la Encarnación (➤ 31)
- Templo de Debod (➤ 25)
- Parque del Oeste (➤ 25)
- Campo del Moro (➤ 29)
- Arab Wall (➤ 60)
- San Andrés (➤ 54)
- Plaza de la Cebada (➤ 52)

INFORMATION

Distance 8km
Time 4–5 hours
Start point Puerta del Sol
cll; D9
Sol (lines 1, 2, 3)
3, 5, 15, 20, 51, 52, 150
End point Puerta del Sol

EVENING STROLLS

MEDIEVAL MADRID

With its hilly, cobbled streets, medieval Madrid is best explored towards sunset when it's at its liveliest. Starting in the Plaza de la Villa, walk southwards via Calle Puñorrostro into the Travesía del Conde. Looking south from here towards Calle Segovia, you will see the Plaza de la Cruz Verde, once used by the Inquisition for *autos da fé*. Crossing Calle Segovia, take the first small street to the right into the Plaza del Alamillo. You are now in the small area of atmospheric, winding streets known as the Morería, or Moorish quarter. From here, go to the Plaza de la Paja, and from there down the Costanilla de San Andrés to the Plaza de San Andrés. Walking up the Costanilla de San Pedro will bring you to the church of San Pedro el Viejo. Café del Nuncio, to the rear of San Pedro, is lovely for an *aperitivo*, particularly between April and October.

THE SALÓN DEL PRADO

Although many buildings in this area can be visited by day, it's fun to come after dark, when many are also illuminated. Start in the Jardin Botánico then walk up the centre of Paseo del Prado, past the Prado Museum as far as the Neptune Fountain in the Plaza Canovas del Castillo. Here turn right up the Calle de Felipe IV and turn right along the back of the Prado Museum to take in San Jerónimo el Real. Continue up past Calle de Felipe IV and past the Casón del Buen Retiro on to Avenida de Alfonso XII. Opposite is the parterre entrance of the Retiro Park – wonderful while there is still daylight but best avoided if there are no people around. Exit the park a little further north and go down Calle Antonio Maura to Plaza de la Lealtad. A little further on is

The Gran Vía, meaning the 'Great Way', lit up

the Neptune Fountain, from which you can either retrace your steps down the Paseo del Prado or cross it and walk up into the Santa Ana area for an evening drink.

ORGANISED SIGHTSEEING

JULIA TOURS

Offers *Artistic Madrid* and *Sightseeing Madrid* tours in English, as well as tours to the major sights in the surrounding area, including Toredo and El Escorial. The Scala Meliá (➤ 82) has its own visit. Tours from 2,700ptas to 13,200ptas.

🔛 bI; D8 ✉ Gran Via 68 ☎ 91 559 96 05 🕐 Mon–Sat 8–8; 8–noon 🚇 Santo Domingo

MADRID VISION

Runs five buses a day around all the major sights. Starting points include Gran Via (➤ 59), the Plaza de España (➤ 52), the Royal Palace (➤ 29), the Puerta del Sol (➤ 35) and the Calle de Serrano (➤ 70). A ticket allowing you to get on and off as often as you wish in a day costs a little more than the ordinary tour price. Panoramic tour 1,200pts (half day), 2,500pts (full day). All major tours are available in English.

🔛 G1 ✉ Avienda di Manoteras 22–91 ☎ 91 767 1743

TRAPSATUR

Offers half and full day tours in English. The *Panorámica y Toros* (3,000ptas) tour takes in a bullfight during the bullfighting season. The company also offers many excursions to locations such as Aranjuez and Chinchón (➤ 20), El Escorial (➤ 20), Segovia (➤ 21) and Toledo (➤ 21).

🔛 bI; D8 ✉ Calle San Bernardo 23 ☎ 91 541 63 20/21 or 542 66 66 🚇 Santo Domingo

PULLMANTOUR

Pullmantour offers an *Artistic* (5,200ptas) tour including the Royal Palace (➤ 29), Calle Mayor (➤ 59), the Puerta del Sol (➤ 35), the Prado Museum (➤ 41) and a *Sightseeing* tour, which visits the Parque del Oeste (➤ 25), Casa de Campo (➤ 57) and the Santiago Bernabeu football stadium among other sights. Prices range from 2,750ptas to 10,000ptas. There are also excursions to Aranjuez and Chinchón (➤ 20), El Escorial (➤ 20), Segovia (➤ 21) and Toledo (➤ 21). All tours are available in English. Prices from 5,000ptas to 10,700ptas.

🔛 alII; C9 ✉ Plaza de Oriente 8 ☎ 91 541 18 05/6/7 🚇 Opera

Made-to-measure sightseeing at low prices

If you are a more adventurous sightseer and armed with a good map and guidebook take a ride on the Circular bus route. It puts you within walking distance of many of Madrid's more important locations, and gives you a good idea of the different *barrios* that make up the whole. Good pick-up points are in the Avenida Menéndez y Pelayo (near the Retiro Park), the Glorieta Emperador Carlos V (near the Prado Museum, the Reina Sofía and the Thyssen), and the Cuesta de San Vicente (near the Parque del Oeste). The round trip takes between 1 and 2 hours, depending on traffic and costs only 130ptas.

EXCURSIONS

INFORMATION

Aranjuez and Chinchón
Distance 45km
Journey time 45 minutes
🕐 Mon–Fri 10–2, 3–5; Sat 10–2
🚌 ALSA from Estación Sur, Méndez Alvaro ☎ 91 468 42 00
🚆 Cercanías Line or the pleasant Tren de la Fresa (Strawberry Train ➤ 58)
💰 Expensive
ℹ️ Plaza San Antonio ☎ 91 891 04 27

El Escorial
Distance 40km
Journey time 45 minutes
☎ 91 890 59 03/4, 866 02 38
🕐 Tue–Sun 10–6; Oct–Mar 10–5
🚌 Autocares Herranz, from outside Moncloa metro station. Buy your ticket here
🚆 Regular trains from Atocha
💰 Expensive
❓ Last admission 1 hour before closing

Awe-inspiring El Escorial

ARANJUEZ & CHINCHÓN

Aranjuez was the Spanish Bourbon monarchy's attempt to create a Spanish Versailles. Inside the royal palace, highlights are the Porcelain Room, the Throne Room and the Smoking Room. The gardens, laid out in the 16th century, include a section called El Jardín de la Isla (Island Garden). A little further afield there is the immense Jardín del Príncipe (Prince's Garden), crisscrossed with shady walkways. At the far end stands the Casa del Labrador (Peasant's House) built for Charles IV. Nearby Chinchón has a 15th-century castle and a wonderful Plaza Mayor, lined with balconied houses. There is a Goya panel in the Assumption Church. Chinchón is the home of the eponymous anise liqueur.

EL ESCORIAL

Philip II's vast palace and monastery was built in the Doric style between 1563 and 1584. Measuring 205m from north to south and 160m from east to west, it contains 16 courtyards, 2,673 windows, 1,200 doors and 86 staircases; 900m of frescos line the walls. Its power is breathtaking, and the clear mountain air has left its granite and blue roof slates looking extraordinarily new. Amongst the highlights are the monastery, the library and the mausoleum, the resting place of most Spanish monarchs since Charles V. Further north is the controversial Valle de los Caídos built by Republican prisoners – General Franco's resting place and a monument to all those who died in the Civil War.

Alcázar, the fortress at Segovia

SEGOVIA

Less touristy than Toledo, Segovia was founded during the Iberian period. It was taken in 80BC by the Romans and became the seat of a bishop under the Visigoths. Occupied by the Moors, it then reverted to the Christians in 1085, and now, a millennium later, it is a popular weekend destination for *madrileños* in search of fresh air and a traditional suckling pig lunch. The first thing you see on entering the town is the Roman aqueduct (1st and 2nd centuries AD), with 165 arches, a total length of 813m, and maximum height of 128m. In the old town are the magnificent 16th-century cathedral and the 14th-century Alcázar, or fortress, from the top of which there are lovely views. Well-known as the capital of Catalan cuisine, Segovia is noted for the quality of its delicious meat dishes. The tender roast lamb and suckling pig are excellent.

TOLEDO

Toledo, one of the most beautiful and legendary cities in Spain, was the Spanish capital under the Visigoths (567–711), and from 1085 until 1561 when Philip II transferred the Spanish Court to Madrid. In other words, it has played a decisive role in Spanish history for far longer than Madrid itself. Between the 12th and 15th centuries Moors and Christians lived there side by side, and its rich combination of Christian, Moorish and Jewish legacies earned it a designation as a National Monument. It is a fascinating maze of winding streets and hidden patios, and its hilltop position affords wonderful views in every direction. Particular highlights are the stunning 13th-century cathedral, the synagogue, the Casa de El Greco (the house of the Greek religious painter whose name is associated with the city) and the Alcázar, or fort, originally founded in 1085, which sits astride the town. To get the most out of Toledo, it is best to stay two days.

INFORMATION

Segovia

Distance 88km

Journey time 2 hours

🚌 La Sepulveda bus line from Paseo de la Florida 11, near Príncipe Pío metro station

🚆 From Chamartín station (very slow)

🍴 Candido, Plaza Azoguejo 5; Restaurante La Almuraza, Calle Marqués del Arco 3

ℹ️ Plaza Mayor 10 ☎ 91 921 46 03 34. The office on Plaza Azoguejo ☎ 91 921 46 03 34 offers information on the surrounding region

Toledo

Distance 50km

Journey time 1 hour 15 minutes

🚌 Galeano International from Estación Sur, Méndez Alvaro ☎ 91 468 42 00

🚆 From Atocha, several every hour in summer, less frequent in winter

ℹ️ Puerta Bisagra ☎ 91 925 22 08 43, on the north side of Toledo

21

WHAT'S ON

January

Cabalgata de Reyes (5 Jan): Procession through streets announces the coming of the Three Wise Men to Madrid's children.

San Antón (17 Jan): Hundreds of people congregate in the San Antón Church, Calle Hortaleza 63, to have their pets blessed.

February

Carnival: The week before Lent, processions and parties, ending on Ash Wednesday with the ritual known as the Burial of the Sardine by the River Manzanares.

ARCO : International contemporary arts festival.

April

Semana Santa (Holy Week): Hooded, shoeless, chain-dragging *penitentes* bear images of Christ and the Virgin on their shoulders. On Holy Thursday during the procession around La Latina, the entire *barrio* takes to the streets.

May

Labour Day and *Madrid Day* (1–2 May): Concerts all over the Madrid region from rock to classical to folk. The centrepiece is in Plaza Mayor and always involves someone famous nationally.

San Isidro (15 May): The week leading up to the saint's day of Madrid's patron, San Isidro, is centred around the Plaza Mayor, with nightly concerts. On the Sunday before the 15th, a huge traditional *cocido* is served, with everyone wearing traditional dress. This is the most important part of Madrid's bullfighting year.

June

St Antonio (13 Jun): Madrid's biggest street party takes place on St Antonio's feast day.

August

Verbenas: Open-air saint's day celebrations in the area around La Latina and Lavapiés; the streets of the *barrio popular* are busy until the small hours.

September–November

Festival de Otoño (Autumn Festival): International performing arts festival.

September–October

Música en las Ventas: National and foreign contemporary musical acts in the bullring.

December

Feria de Artesanía: This annual craft fair takes place in the Paseo de Recoletos in the weeks leading up to Christmas. There's also a Christmas fair in the Plaza Mayor.

New Year's Eve: Thousands of *madrileños* gather in the Puerta del Sol to see the fireworks. At midnight the ritual is to eat one grape for each of the clock's 12 chimes.

MADRID's
top 25 sights

*The sights are shown on the maps on the inside front cover and inside back cover, numbered **1–25** from west to east across the city*

ERMITA DE SAN ANTONIO

Goya is surely the painter whom most madrileños *want to claim as their own. The San Antonio Hermitage, a National Monument, is the finest memorial the city could have raised to his memory.*

HIGHLIGHTS

- Cupola
- Balustrade
- Marble and stucco font (1798)
- Lápida de Goya
- Mirrors under the cupola
- High altar
- Lamp under the cupola (18th century)
- *Inmaculada* by Jacinto Gómez Pastor
- *San Luis and San Isidro,* Jacinto Gómez Pastor

INFORMATION

- B8
- Glorieta de San Antonio de la Florida 5
- 91 542 07 22
- Tue–Fri 10–2, 4–8. Sat and Sun 10–2. Closed public hols
- Norte
- 41, 46, 75
- Norte Station
- None
- Inexpensive. Free Wed and Sun
- Parque del Oeste (➤ 25)
- Guide book sold at entrance

History Both church and hermitage – the latter to the right as you face the two buildings – are off the beaten track but worthwhile both for their intimacy and to view Goya's frescos, restored in 1990. The original hermitage was begun in 1792 by Charles IV's Italian architect, Francisco Fontana, on the site of a previous hermitage. Goya's remains were buried here in 1919, unfortunately without his head: rumour has it that it was stolen by scientists who wished to study it.

The frescos Painted using a technique that was revolutionary at the time, the frescos are distinguished by their richness of colour. They tell the life of Saint Anthony, representing the saint raising a murdered man from the dead to enable him to name his murderer and spare the life of the innocent accused. The models for the frescos were members of the Spanish Court, but include other, less reputable figures – placing rogues alongside the Court officials has been seen as indicating Goya's contempt for the Court of the time.

Girlfriends and boyfriends The San Antonio Hermitage is locally considered particularly *castizo* (of the people), and it is the focal point of a peculiar ritual. Saint Anthony is the patron saint of sweethearts; every 13 June, girls come here to pray for a boyfriend. Thirteen pins are placed inside the font; when the girls put their hands into the font, the number of pins that stick indicates how many boyfriends they will have that year.

PARQUE DEL OESTE

Less frequented and more informal than the Retiro, the Parque del Oeste is the best place in the city for a peaceful, summer twilight stroll, particularly at its quieter northern end.

History Originally designed in the first years of the 20th century by landscape gardener Cecilio Rodríguez on what had previously been an immense rubbish heap, the Parque del Oeste was practically destroyed during the Civil War when it provided a cover for the Rebuplicans as the Nationalist troops invaded Madrid. Now rebuilt, it is still one of the city's most appealing and romantic open spaces, despite the best efforts of litter louts and graffiti artist. The park contains birch, fir, atlas cedar and cypress trees among others, as well as a 17,000-sq m rose garden, La Rosaleda, which hosts a rose festival each May. There are also several statues, including the 1952 Juan Villanueva fountain in the Paseo de Camoens. A *teleférico* (cable car) in the park runs out to the Casa de Campo, affording bird's-eye views over the west of Madrid. In summer, elegant, noisy terrace bars are set up along the Paseo de Pintor Rosales, Ernest Hemingway's favourite street.

Templo de Debod It is somehow typical of Madrid that one of its oddest and most interesting attractions should not be Spanish at all: the Debod Temple, on the site of a former military barracks in a little park of its own at the southern corner near Playa de España, is a 4th-century Egyptian temple honouring the god Amon. It was installed in 1970 as a gift from the Egyptian government to Spanish engineers and archaeologists who had saved many valuable artistic treasures before large areas of land were flooded by the construction of the Aswan Dam.

HIGHLIGHTS

- Templo de Debod
- *Teleférico*
- La Rosaleda
- Fuente (fountain)
- Statue of Juan de Villanueva
- Statue of Sor Juana Inés de la Cruz
- Statue of Simón Bolívar
- View over Casa de Campo
- Trees, including atlas cedar, cypress and magnolia

INFORMATION

- ✚ B7
- ✉ Jardines del Paseo del Pintor Rosales
- ☎ 91 409 61 65
- ◷ (Templo de Debod): Tue–Fri 10–2, 6–8;. Sat and Sun 10–2. Closed public hols
- ☺ Plaza de España, Ventura Rodriguez, Moncloa
- ☐ 74, 84, 93
- ⓦ Templo de Debod: Inexpensive. Free Wed and Sun
- ↔ Ermita de San Antonio (► 24)

Top: the Debod Temple

3

MUSEO DE AMÉRICA

HIGHLIGHTS

- Sculptures of people with physical defects (Area 3)
- Canoe and tepee (Area 3)
- Statues of tribal chieftains (Area 3)
- Painting of *Entrance of Viceroy Morcillo into Potosí* (Area 3)
- Shrunken heads (Area 4)
- Portable altar-piece (Area 4)
- Mummy of Parácas (Area 4)
- Treasure of the Quimbayas (Area 4)
- 'Day of the Dead' paraphernalia (Area 4)
- Trocortesiano Maya Codex (Area 5)

INFORMATION

- ➕ C6
- ✉ Avenida Reyes Católicos 6
- ☎ 91 543 94 37
- 🕐 Tue–Sat 10–3; Sun and public hols 10–2.30
- Ⓜ Moncloa
- 🚌 Circular, 82, 83, 84.
- 🎫 Inexpensive. Free Sun
- ♿ Excellent

Vessel from Peru

This attractive museum is the best place in Spain to absorb the flavour of the culture of a different continent. It makes a unique contribution to Spanish cultural life.

History Situated on the edge of Madrid's sprawling University City area, the America Museum is devoted to the presentation and explication of Pre-Columbian and Hispanic artefacts from Latin America. Depending on your point of view, you may see it either as an attempt to promote international understanding or as propaganda for the Spanish Conquest. The collection was housed in part of the Archaeological Museum until 1993, when it took its present form. Tragically, much of the material brought back between Columbus's first voyage and the mid-17th century was destroyed in successive palace fires, and more of the exhibits were brought back to Spain by scientists, or given as donations, than had been by the *conquistadores*.

Layout The only information in English is a small pamphlet available at the entrance. Do yourself a favour and follow the suggested route as it is easy to get confused and have a less enjoyable experience. The collection is spread over two floors and five areas with different themes: the tools of understanding, the reality of America's society, religion and communication. Audio-visual aids are available in Spanish. Two particular highlights are the Treasure of the Quimbayas (Area 4), including exquisite gold figures, skullcap helmets, drinking flasks and trumpets from Columbia, and the Trocortesiano Maya codex (Area 5), which records the arrival of the Spaniards in the New World and the Spanish Conquest in minute, intricate runes.

4

MUSEO CERRALBO

Idiosyncratic and intermittently splendid, this real curiosity shows you how the nobility of Madrid lived 100 years ago, and in particular the extravagant personality of the aristocrat, the Marquis de Cerralbo.

History When you seen the two-storey, late 19th-century home of the 17th Marquis of Cerralbo from the outside it looks rather unpromising. But the clutter of artefacts inside is fascinating, and uniquely among the house-museums in Madrid, the collections are rivalled by the architecture and decor of the rooms themselves, ranging from the frankly shabby to the magnificent. Politician, man of letters and collector, the Marquis donated the house and its contents to the state in 1922, stipulating that his collection be displayed exactly as he had left it. This is a unique opportunity to see a near-intact aristocrat's home of the turn of the 20th century.

The collection A magnificent grand staircase by Soriano Fort is to your right as you enter. On the first floor the most notable exhibit is El Greco's striking *Ecstasy of St Francis* (1600–5) in the chapel. In the gallery surrounding the patio there are works by José de Ribera and Alonso Cano as well as some haunting Alessandro Magnasco landscapes. On the second floor there are collections of Western and oriental weaponry, a dining-room containing a remarkable Frans Snyders painting, and an appealingly cosy library. Pride of place is given to the sumptuous, mirrored ballroom on the ground floor, which displays the Marquis' Saxon porcelain as well as intricately engineered clocks, including one particularly fascinating and enormous specimen. Note that tours and information are in Spanish only.

HIGHLIGHTS

- Grand staircase
- *Ecstasy of St Francis*, El Greco
- *Jacob with his Flock*, Jusepe Ribera
- *Devotion*, Alonso Cano
- *Immaculate Conception*, Francisco Zurbarán
- *Porcupines and Snakes*, Frans Snyders
- Sword collection from the courts of Louis XV and XVI
- Porcelain Room
- Ballroom
- Monumental mystery clock

INFORMATION

- C8
- Calle Ventura Rodríguez 17
- 91 547 36 46
- Tue–Sat 9:30–7:30; Sun 10–2. Closed Aug and public hols
- Ventura Rodríguez, Plaza de España.
- 1, 46, 74, 75
- Inexpensive. Free Sun and Wed
- Parque del Oeste (➤ 25)
- Few

Top: the Salón de Baile

CATEDRAL LA ALMUDENA

Though not the world's prettiest cathedral, it is a record of years of Spanish architectural thought. The mixture of styles demonstrates how casual madrileños have been about this building, which you would expect to have been a high priority.

A long delay Incredible though it may seem, a few years ago Madrid lacked a cathedral. The first plans for the Almudena, constructed on what was formerly the site of Muslim Madrid's principal mosque, were drawn up in 1879 under Alfonso XII by the architect Giambattista Sacchetti. Redesigned in 1883, it is based on the pattern of a 13th-century cathedral, with a chancel similar to the one at Rheims. A neo-classical style was introduced into the design in 1944 by architect, Fernado Chueca Goitia, but financial problems delayed completion of the cloister until 1955, with the façade following five years later. The crypt alone took 30 years to complete. It wasn't until 1993, when the the final touches were added, that the cathedral was finally consecrated by the Pope. The main entrance is opposite the Royal Palace, while the entrance to the crypt is along La Cuesta de la Vega.

The story of the Almudena Virgin According to legend, the image of the Virgin over the entrance had been hidden in the 11th century by Mozarabs (Jews and Christians living under Moorish rule). When Spanish hero El Cid reconquered Madrid and drove the Moors out, he ordered that the image be found, but without success. When Alfonso VI arrived in Madrid, he instructed his troops and the people of Madrid to dismantle the city walls to find the image. When they reached the grain deposits, they heard a noise from the turrets above, which then collapsed, revealing an image of the Virgin and Child.

DID YOU KNOW?

- Almudaina means 'small walled city' in Arabic
- Almudit means 'grain store'
- Alfonso XII laid the first stone in 1883
- Crypt is built of stone from Portugal
- Image of the Virgin is made of pinewood
- There are 600 columns in the crypt
- Partly built with money from noble families buying their own chapels
- There are 20 chapels: 9 on the right, 11 on the left
- On the crypt floor some blank tombstones still await an owner

INFORMATION

- ✚ all; C9
- ✉ Calle Bailén. Next to Palacio Real
- ☎ 91 542 22 00
- ◷ Daily 10–1:30, 6–7:45
- Ⓜ Opera
- 🚌 3, 31, 148
- 🎟 Free
- ↔ Palacio Real (➤ 29), Plaza del Oriente (➤ 30)
- ♿ None

6

PALACIO REAL

The scale of the Royal Palace is undeniably awesome and the sheer pomp is a little overwhelming. The story that sentries guarding the rear of the building used to freeze to death in the icy wind adds to the sense of chilliness it inspires.

History Also known as the Palacio de Oriente or the Palacio Nacional, the Royal Palace was begun under Philip V in 1737 after the old Muslim fortress had been destroyed by fire in 1734. The original design by Filippo Juvara was for façades measuring 476m each, or three times longer than the palace as it is now, but there was neither the space nor the money for it. It was not completed until 1764 and designed by Sacchetti. From the street side, it is a normal palatial building of the period, with Doric pilasters framing the reception hall windows. The royal family does not actually live here: it is used occasionally for state visits, during which dinner is served in the gala dining room. The entrance is to the south side of the building, across the Plaza de la Armería, which is flanked by the Royal Armoury housing El Cid's sword and suits of armour.

Interior and gardens Most of the more than 3,000 rooms are never used. A ceiling by Conrado Giaquinto accents the grand staircase. The ceiling of the Sala de Gasperini is remarkable, done in stucco, while the ceiling of the Sala de Porcelana, built for Charles III, has a fine display of white, gold and green porcelain plaques. To the north of the palace are the elegant Sabatini Gardens, which offer the best view of the palace, while to the rear is the Campo del Moro (Moor's Field), with a splendid Carriage Museum. The only way to see the palace is by a guided tour, which takes in the most impressive rooms.

HIGHLIGHTS

- Grand staircase
- Sala de Porcelana
- Salón de Alabarderos
- Salón de Columnas
- Saleta de Gasparini
- Salón de Carlos III
- Clock collection
- Chapel by Giambattista Sacchetti and Ventura Rodriguez
- Music Museum
- Sabatini Gardens

INFORMATION

- ✚ all; C9
- ✉ Calle Bailén
- ☎ 91 542 00 59
- 🕐 Mon–Sat 9:30–5; Sun and public hols 9–2
- Ⓜ Opera
- 🚌 3, 25, 33, 148
- ✋ Moderate
- ↔ Catedral la Almudena (➤ 28)
- ♿ Very good

Philip II, by the Royal Palace

MADRID
A
FELIPE II

PLAZA DE ORIENTE

DID YOU KNOW?

- General Franco held mass rallies here
- Tunnels beneath the square date back to Moorish times
- Earliest royal with statue: King Ataulfo (AD 415)
- Statue of Philip IV is at the geometrical centre of square
- Statues brought to square in 1841
- Previous location of Philip IV was Buen Retiro Palace
- Equestrian statue weighs 7,500kg
- First performance in Royal Theatre was Donizetti's *The Favourite*

INFORMATION

- ✚ all; C9
- ✉ Plaza de Oriente
- 🍴 Café de Oriente
- Ⓜ Opera
- 🚌 3, 25, 33
- ↔ Palacio Real (➤ 29), Monasterio de la Encarnación (➤ 31)

Have an aperitivo on the terrace of the Café de Oriente, with the harmonious formal gardens stretching away in front of you to the Royal Palace. This is undoubtedly the best place to reflect on the might of the monarchy at the height of its powers.

Ambitious emperor The elegant Plaza de Oriente was planned in 1811 under Joseph Bonaparte. To build it, he had to destroy the monuments and churches that then surrounded the Royal Palace. His original aim had been to build a kind of Champs Élysées, running from the Plaza to the Cibeles Fountain. Fortunately, the Champs Élysées project was abandoned; had it not been, Madrid would have lost, among many other treasures, the Convent of the Royal Shoeless Nuns. The existing square dates from the reign of Queen Isabella II (1833–1904). The attractively laid-out gardens contain statues of the kings and queens of Spain, which were originally intended for the top of the Royal Palace facing on to the plaza, but were never put into place because they were too heavy and Isabella II dreamed that an earthquake made them topple over on to her.

Teatro Real At the eastern end of the square stands the Royal Theatre, built between 1818 and 1850 and now restored. The open-air theatre that originally occupied the site was expanded in 1737 for a visit by Farinelli, the legendary *castrato* singer, of whom Philip V (1683–1746) was particularly fond. It reopened in 1997, after ten years' refurbishment, on the Saint's Day of Queen Isabella II, its founder.

The horse The equestrian statue in the centre of the square is of Philip IV by Montañes, taken from a portrait by Velázquez.

8

MONASTERIO DE LA ENCARNACIÓN

Located away from the traffic of Calle Bailén, the Monastery of the Incarnation is the monumental equivalent of a tranquilliser, suffused with religious calm that brings peace to the soul.

History Designed by Juan Gómez de Mora in 1611 on instructions from Queen Margarita, wife of Philip III, the church in the Royal Monastery is a typical example of Habsburg Spanish religious architecture. Originally the monastery was connected by a secret passage to the Arab fortress where the Royal Palace now stands. The church was damaged by fire in 1734, and reconstructed by Ventura Rodríguez in a classical-baroque style in the 1760s; the granite façade is all that remains of the original. A 45-minute guided tour leads you through the monastery, which is still used by nuns of the Augustine order; you see the Royal Room, hung with fairly uninspired portraits of the Spanish royal family and one of Madrid's most beautiful churches, the monastery church, which includes the reliquary. The church houses the lesser-known of Madrid's two monastery museums (the other being the Descalzas Reales).

The Reliquary At the its centre stands an altar and altar-piece with a panel depicting the Holy Family by Bernadino Luini, a pupil of Leonardo da Vinci and an ornate tabernacle in bronze and rock crystal. Inside is a crucifix of Christ with a crown of thorns, oddly charred: tradition holds that these are the remains of a crucifix that was defiled and burnt by heretics. Among the 1,500 relics on display the most noteworthy object, in a small glass globe to the right of the door as you enter, is the dried blood of St Pantaleón, which mysteriously liquefies for 24 hours beginning at midnight every 27 July, St Pantaleón's Day.

HIGHLIGHTS

- *John the Baptist*, Jusepe Ribera
- *Handing over of the Princesses*, anonymous painting in lobby
- *Recumbent Christ*, Perronius
- Royal Room
- Altar-piece
- Cupola, with frescos by González Velázquez
- Frescos: Francisco Bayeu
- Charred crucifix
- Blood of St Pantaleón

INFORMATION

- ✚ al; C8
- ✉ Plaza de la Encarnación 1
- ☎ 91 542 00 59
- ◉ Monastery and Reliquary Wed, Sat 10:30–2.30, 4–6:30; Sun 11–2:30
- ◎ Opera
- ▭ 3, 148
- 🎫 Inexpensive. Free Wed
- ↔ Catedral la Almudena (➤ 28), Palacio Real (➤ 29)
- ♿ None

PLAZA DE LA VILLA

HIGHLIGHTS

- Statue of Admiral Alvaro de Bazán
- Staircase of Honour (Casa del Ayuntamiento)
- Statue of Goya (Casa del Ayuntamiento)
- Visiting Room, with engraving of oldest map of Madrid (1622) (Casa del Ayuntamiento)
- Glass patio (Casa del Ayuntamiento)
- Tapestry Room, with 15th-century pieces (Casa de Cisneros)
- Commissions Gallery

INFORMATION

- all; D9
- Plaza de la Villa
- 91 588 29 06/08
- Buildings open Mon 5–6
- Sol, Opera
- 3
- Free
- Plaza Mayor (➤ 33), Puerta del Sol (➤ 35)
- Spanish guide only for buildings. With advance phone call, guided tours in French and English can be arranged for groups
- None

The small scale of this typically Castilian and perfectly rectangular square makes a pleasant change from some of the more imposing buildings in Madrid. Here you will see three different architectural styles in harmonious co-existence.

Casa del Ayuntamiento Dramatically floodlit at night, the plaza has been the venue for Madrid Town Council meetings since 1405. Originally the site of an Arab street market, it is now the home to three buildings in three distinct styles. The Casa del Ayuntamiento, sometimes referred to as la Casa de la Villa, is Castilian-baroque. It was designed in 1640 by Juan Gómez de Mora, the first to introduce rectangular forms to the Madrid landscape, with two doors, one for the Council and one for the prison that also occupied the building. The existing doors are baroque modifications, dating from 1670. The building's façade was later altered by Juan de Villanueva in 1787, and a balcony leading on to the Plaza Mayor was added. Inside is a grand staircase and a room containing a painting by Goya.

Two fine buildings The much-restored Casa de Cisneros, on the south side of the square, is one of Madrid's finest examples of the Plateresque style prevalent in the 16th century. It was built as a palace by a relative of the great Cardinal Cisneros in 1537. The Torre de los Lujanes, the third noteworthy structure on the square, is one of the few monuments in Madrid surviving from the 15th century; it is a fine example of late Gothic civic architecture. It was the residence of one of Madrid's aristocratic families from the 1460s and it is said that King Francis I of France was held prisoner here in 1525 by Hernando de Alarcón, who owned the house at the time.

PLAZA MAYOR

The cobbled Plaza Mayor strikes a chord with everyone entering it for the first time: it's here that you fully realise you are in the capital of Spain. Surely it is only in Madrid that the early 1990s frescos on the façade of Casa Panadería could have survived.

History Built in the 15th century as a market square, and later renamed the Plaza del Arrabal (Square outside the Walls), the Plaza Mayor came into its own when Philip II, after making Madrid the capital of Spain, ordered it to be rebuilt as the administrative centre of the Court. The only part to be completed immediately was the Panadería, or the bakery, by architect Drego Sillero in 1590 (the frescos are the work of the early 1990s), while the rest of it was completed in 1619 by architect Juan Gómez de la Mora under Philip III, whose bronze equestrian statue (by Juan de Bolonia and Pietro Tacca) stands at the centre. After fire in 1790 much of the square had to be rebuilt. The buildings between the towers on either side of the square are Town Hall offices; the rest are private residences.

A gathering place During the 17th century, the Plaza Mayor was where the more important members of the Court lived. At the end of the century, the square became the site of bullfights, carnivals and the terrible *autos da fé* of the Spanish Inquisition, which were attended by thousands on 30 June 1680, when 118 of the offenders were executed in a single day. Hangings were carried out here until the end of the 18th century. To this day the plaza is the scene of many public gatherings.

DID YOU KNOW?

- Number of arches: 114
- Number of balconies: 377
- Square measures 120 x 90m
- Shop at No. 4 opened in 1790
- Seven 'Juans' have played a part in the square's history
- Three destructive fires, in 1631, 1672 and 1790
- Philip II statue was gift from Duke of Florence
- Official name of square is Plaza de la Constitución

INFORMATION

- bII; D9
- Plaza Mayor
- *Terraza* bars around square
- Sol
- 3, 5, 150
- Plaza de la Villa (► 32)
- Tourist office in square

A good place to watch the world go by

CONVENTO DE LAS DESCALZAS REALES

HIGHLIGHTS

- *Recumbent Christ,* Gaspar Becerra
- *Neapolitan Nativity* (Chapel of St Michael)
- *Virgin of the Forsaken,* Tomás Yepes
- *St Ursula and the Eleven Thousand Virgins,* Giulio Lucini
- Bust of the *Mater Dolorosa,* José Risueño
- *Cardinal Infante Don Fernando of Austria,* Rubens
- *The Ship of the Church,*16th-century painting
- *Adoration of the Magi,* Brueghel
- *The Empress Maria,* Goya Church

INFORMATION

- ✠ bl–bll; D9
- ✉ Plaza de las Descalzas Reales 3
- ☎ 91 542 00 59
- ⏰ Tue, Wed, Thu, Sat 10:30–12:45, 4–5:45; Fri 10:30–12:45; Sun and public hols 11–1:45
- 🚇 Sol, Callao
- 🚌 3, 5, 150
- ♿ None
- 💷 Moderate. Free Wed
- ↔ Puerta del Sol, Real Academia de Bellas Artes de San Fernando (➤ 35, 36)

Top: Recumbent Christ, *by Becerra*

Though the tour of the Royal Shoeless Nuns' Convent is conducted at a frenetic pace, the building contains an unusually high proportion of unmissable treasures and it merits more than one return trip.

Convent history Of Madrid's two monastery museums, the Descalzas Reales is the richest. Oddly located in the centre of commercial Madrid, it is a small miracle that it remains intact; most of its rooms are small museums in themselves. Founded by Juana of Austria, the younger daughter of Charles V, on the site of the place in which she was born, it was built between 1559 and 1564 in Madrid brick by Antonio Silla and Juan Bautista of Toledo. The church was completed in 1570 by Diego de Villanueva. The whole place breathes mid-17th-century religious mysticism, though the 'vile stink' or unpleasant smell of which traveller William Beckford complained when attending Mass here in the late 18th century has departed. The original sisters were all of noble or aristocratic blood, and each founded a chapel on reception into the order: there are 33 of them, and to this day the convent is home to 33 Franciscan nuns, each of whom maintains one of the chapels.

The art collection The tour of the convent takes in a quarter of the rooms. Given in Spanish only, it lasts around 45 minutes and is conducted at such a frenzied pace that it is worth buying a guide book at the entrance. Unfortunately you cannot go around independently. The Grand Staircase, with its *trompe l'oeil* portrait of Philip IV and his family standing on the balcony, is covered with frescos by the artist Claudio Coello. The church can be visited only during Mass, at 8AM or 7PM.

PUERTA DEL SOL

Almost inevitably in Madrid, you will cross this square several times. For many madrileños, *it is the true soul of the city and each year thousands of* madrileños *gather here to see in the New Year.*

Soul of Madrid The area's namesake gateway was demolished in 1570 when the square was widened to receive Anne of Austria, Philip II's fourth wife. The design of the square dates back to 1861, the building on the south side, the Casa de Correos, is from 1768. Originally the Post Office, it is now the headquarters of the Madrid regional government. Spain's Kilometre Zero, the point from which all distances in Spain are measured, can be found on the pavement in front of it. The clock and tower were built in 1867.

A troubled history It was in Sol that the Esquilache mutiny of 1766 began, sparked by Charles III's uncharacteristically tyrannical insistence that the population should wear short capes and three-cornered hats to emulate a hated French style. The most notable moment in Sol's history was on 2 and 3 May 1808, when the *madrileños* took up arms against invading French troops, a heroic resistance in which more than 2,000 died. Both days are immortalised in Goya's two magnificent anti-war paintings in the Prado, *The Second of May* and *The Third of May*. Various 20th-century uprisings also took place in Sol: it was here that politician José Canalejas was assassinated 1912, and the Second Republic was proclaimed in 1931. It remains a popular meeting place in Madrid, especially by the monument of the bear with a strawberry tree.

HIGHLIGHTS

- Bear and *madroño* (strawberry tree) statue
- Statue of Charles III
- La Mallorquina pastry shop
- Newspaper stands: a major part of Madrid street-life
- Tío Pepe sign ('Andalusian Sunshine in a Bottle')
- Kilometre Zero
- Doña Manolita's lottery ticket stalls

INFORMATION

- cll; D9
- Puerta del Sol
- Sol
- 3, 5, 15, 20, 51, 52, 150
- Plaza Mayor (➤ 33), Convento de las Descalzas Reales (➤ 34), Real Academia de Bellas Artes (➤ 36)

Statue of the bear with a strawberry tree

REAL ACADEMIA DE BELLAS ARTES

HIGHLIGHTS

- Goya self-portraits (Room 20)
- *The Burial of the Sardine*, Goya (Room 20)
- *Alonso Rodríguez*, Francisco Zurbarán (Room 6)
- *Christ Crucified*, Alonso Cano (Room 3)
- *Head of John the Baptist*, Jusepe Ribera (Room 3)
- *Felipe IV*, Velázquez (Room 11)
- *Susana and the Elders*, Rubens (Room 13)
- *Spring*, Guiseppe Arcimboldo (Room 14)
- *Martyrdom of S Bartolome*, Ribera (Room 3)
- Goya etchings (Calcografía Nacional)

INFORMATION

- cII; D9
- Calle Alcalá 13
- 91 522 14 91
- Tue–Fri 9–7; Sat, Sun, Mon and public hols 9–2:30
- Sol, Sevilla
- 3, 5, 15, 20, 51, 52, 150
- Inexpensive. Free Sat and Sun
- Convento de las Descalzas Reales (➤ 34), Puerta del Sol (➤ 35)
- Good

Though often passed over in favour of the big three – the Prado, the Thyssen and the Reina Sofía – the stately and graceful Royal Academy of Fine Arts is interesting to visit, containing work by major artists rejected by the Prado and the Thyssen.

History It was Francisco Meléndez who suggested the establishment of a Royal Academy on the model of those in Rome, Paris and Florence and other great cities. Work began on the authorisation of Philip V in 1744 and was completed under Fernando VI in 1752. The Academy was initially in the Casa de la Panadería, in the Plaza Mayor, but Charles III transferred it to its present site in 1773. The original building was baroque, but shortly after it opened, Academy members with conservative tastes insisted that it be given today's neo-classical façade. Rarely overcrowded, it is small enough to be visited comfortably in a couple of days.

Layout The museum has three floors. The best-known galleries are on the first floor, most notably Room 20 containing examples of Goya's work. Other highlights by 17th-century Spanish artists include *Head of John the Baptist* by José de Ribera (1591–1652), *Alonso Rodríguez* by Francisco Zurbarán and *Felipé IV* by Velázquez. Pay particular attention to the 16th-century Milanese painter Giuseppe Arcimboldo's *Spring* in Room 14, it is the only Arcimboldo in Spain and one of only a handful in the world. Halfway up the stairs to the entrance (and easily missed) is another museum, La Calcografía Nacional, or Engraving Plates Museum. The Gabinete Goya at the back of this is a hidden treasure, which contains a beautifully displayed series of the original plates used by the artist for his etchings.

COLECCIÓN THYSSEN-BORNEMISZA

This is one of the best things that has happened to Madrid since the end of the Civil War. It is also one of the few internationally renowned art museums where everything *is priority viewing.*

A new museum The Thyssen, housing what may be the world's finest private art collection, opened its doors to the public in October 1992. At that time the collection was on loan to Spain, but an agreement to purchase it was reached in June 1993 in the face of stiff competition, with the Spanish state agreeing to pay a bid-winning $350 million. The collection was begun by Baron Thyssen's father, who died in 1947. The paintings were dispersed among his heirs, but the Baron bought them back. Continuing to collect himself, and also wishing to keep the collection together, he and his wife Tita Cervera, a former Miss Spain, chose the Palacio de Villahermosa to house the collection.

The collection The sheer variety of the 775 works on display prompted some to call the Thyssen over-eclectic; others believe its very quirkiness is part of its charm. Each room highlights a different period; the top floor is devoted to art from medieval times through to the 17th-century, the first floor to the rococo and neo-classicism of the 18th and 19th centuries, through to fauvism and expressionism, the ground level to 20th-century surrealism, pop art and the avant-garde. Start from the top and work your way down. A free guide book in English is provided.

HIGHLIGHTS

- *Portrait of Giovanna Tornabuoni*, Domenico Ghirlandaio
- *Portrait of Henry VIII*, Holbein
- *St Catherine of Alexandria*, Caravaggio
- *Annunciation Diptych*, Van Eyck
- *St Jerome in the Wilderness*, Titian
- *The Lock*, Constable
- *Easter Morning*, Caspar David Friedrich
- *Les Vessenots*, Van Gogh
- *Houses on the River*, Egon Schiele
- *Man with a Clarinet*, Picasso

INFORMATION

- ✚ dII; E9
- ✉ Paseo del Prado 8
- ☎ 91 420 39 44
  Information 369 01 51
- ◷ Tue–Sun 10–7
- 🍴 Café, restaurant
- Ⓜ Banco de España
- 🚌 1, 2, 5, 9, 10, 14, 15, 20, 27, 34, 37, 45, 51, 52, 53, 74, 146, 150
- 🚇 Atocha, Recoletos
- 💷 Moderate
- ↔ Museo del Prado (▶ 41)
- ❓ Bookshop on ground floor
- ♿ Excellent

King Henry VIII *by Holbein (1497–1543)*

CENTRO NACIONAL DE ARTE REINA SOFÍA

HIGHLIGHTS

- View from exterior lifts
- Enclosed patio
- *Guernica*, Picasso
- Juan Gris Room
- Picasso Room
- Joan Miró Room
- Dalí Room
- Surrealism Room
- Luis Buñuel Room
- Spanish 20th-Century Art Room

INFORMATION

- ➕ dIV; E10
- ✉ Calle Santa Isabel 52
- ☎ 91 467 50 62
- 🕐 Wed–Mon 10–9; Sun 10–2:30
- 🍴 Bar, restaurant
- Ⓜ Atocha
- 🚌 6, 10, 14, 24, 26, 27, 32, 34, 36, 37, 41, 45, 47, 54, 56, 57, 85, 86
- 🚊 Atocha
- 💶 Inexpensive. Free Sat afternoon and Sun morning
- ❓ Excellent shop on ground floor
- ♿ Very good

Top: Picasso's Guernica
Above: external lifts on the Reina Sofía

In Madrid's leading modern art museum, the home of Picasso's Guernica, *you might not like all the works on display, but even on its busiest days the Reina Sofía's light and airy space is a delight.*

A triumph of planning Inspired by the Pompidou Centre in Paris, this 12,505-sq m space is Madrid's finest contemporary art centre and was converted from San Carlos hospital between 1977 and 1986. Indeed, among European museums only the Pompidou is larger. Transparent lifts outside of the building whisk you up for a thrilling view over the

rooftops of Madrid. The permanent collection is devoted to Spanish art of the 20th-century, in all its 'isms' – cubism, surrealism, realism, informalism. Most of the other space here is devoted to temporary exhibitions, which are sometimes considered radically avant-garde.

Guernica Picasso's masterpiece dominates the Reina Sofía. When it was commissioned by the Republican Government for display at the 1937 Paris Exhibition, the only instruction was that it be big: it measures 3.5m by 7m. Taking his inspiration from the Nationalist bombing of the Basque town of Guernica in 1937, this painting has become 20th-century art's great anti-war symbol. Many saw the 1995 decision to remove the bullet-proof screen that had protected it for many years as a symbolic gesture, showing that democracy in Spain had finally taken root.

16

MUSEO SOROLLA

This beautifully serene spot was the effort of Spain's finest impressionist painter, Valencian Joaquín Sorolla, to create an oasis of peace for himself in a busy city. It is the best of Madrid's house museums.

Entrance and gardens The Sorolla Museum is also one of the few places in the city to give us a sense of the shape of an artist's life and work. Built in 1910–11 by Enrique María de Repollés, it was the Madrid home of Joaquín Sorolla (1863–1923) and it became a museum after Sorolla's widow, Clotilde, donated it to the state. It was opened to the public in 1932. The two small gardens, designed by Sorolla himself as a setting for his collection of fountains and fonts, are a little bit of Andalucía in Madrid: the first is an imitation of a part of the Seville *alcázar*, while the second is modelled on the Generalife Gardens in Granada's Alhambra. Near the entrance is a replica of a white marble bust of Sorolla by sculptor Mariano Benlliure, and to the left, opposite the entrance, is an Andalucian patio area.

The house Lovingly preserved, the house has seven rooms on two floors, including a salon and a dining room. Each room is given over to a different aspect of Sorolla's work. Be sure to visit his studio, complete with Turkish bed where he is reputed to have taken his *siesta* every day. Although some see a fairy-tale, picture-postcard quality in his art, there is no denying the brilliance of his use of light, and his eloquent reflection of the leisurely, idyllic world before World War I in which everyone wore white, the sea perpetually sparkled, young women lounged decorously on the grass reading books, and there was never a need to be passionate about anything.

HIGHLIGHTS

- *La Bata Rosa* (Room II)
- *Self Portrait* (Room III)
- *Clotilde en traje de noche* (Room III)
- *Clotilde en traje gris* (Room III)
- Turkish bed, used by Sorolla for siestas (Room III)
- *La Siesta* (Room IV)
- *Las Velas* (Room IV)
- *Nadadores* (Room V)
- *Madre* (Room VI)
- New York gouaches (Drawings Room)

INFORMATION

- ✚ E7
- ✉ Paseo del General Martínez Campos
- ☎ 91 310 15 84
- 🕐 Tue–Sat 10–3; Sun and public hols 10–2
- 🚇 Iglesia, Rubén Darío
- 🚌 5, 7, 16, 40, 61, 147
- 🎫 Inexpensive. Free Sun
- ♿ Few

PLAZA DE LA CIBELES

THE SIGHTS

- Post Office
- Gardens of Palacio de Linares
- Façade of Bank of Spain building
- Post Office clock
- Robert Michel's lions
- Newspaper stand on Paseo del Prado

INFORMATION

- dl; E8
- Plaza de la Cibeles
- Banco de España
- 5, 9, 10, 14, 20, 27, 34, 45, 51, 53
- Atocha, Recoletos
- Museo del Prado (➤ 41), Museo Arqueológico Nacional (➤ 43)

Despite the constant traffic, this plaza is Madrid's most overwhelming, a sheer mass of fashioned stone. Centred on a statue of La Cibeles, the fertility goddess – Madrid's equivalent of the Eiffel Tower.

History Seated imperiously at one of Madrid's busiest intersections, the goddess and her marble fountain were erected according to instructions from Charles III (1716–88). The main statue is by Francisco Gutiérrez and the lions, Hipponomes and Atlanta, by Robert Michel. Originally at the corner of the square it was finally completed in 1792. The statue was moved under the the order of the Duke of Romanones in 1895 at which date the cherubim were added.

Around the Plaza The enormous wedding-cake look-alike on the southeastern side of the square is one of Madrid's most imposing buildings. Visitors are sometimes disappointed to discover that it is only the Central Post Office – often dubbed as Our Lady of Communications by local wits. It was designed by Antonio Palacios in 1904, a painstakingly worked façade reminiscent of the Viennese style.

The Palacio de Linares The real treasure of the Plaza de la Cibeles is the Palacio de Linares (which is said to be haunted). It was designed in 1872 by architect Carlos Collubi, and restored and opened in 1992 as the Casa de América and as a gesture of goodwill on the 500th anniversary of Columbus's discovery of America. The beautifully lit interior now showcases exhibits about Latin American visual arts. It also offers music, theatre performances and lectures. The garden is elegantly laid out, and in the summer there is an excellent café-restaurant.

Top: Central Post Office
Above: La Cibeles statue

MUSEO DEL PRADO

The city's pride in the magnificent Prado is justified. With its bounty of Goyas, El Grecos and other masterpieces, it is one of the world's great museums, despite its haughty and magnificently frustrating indifference to visitors.

Brief history Some people still believe that Madrid is a one-sight city, and that that sight is the Prado, a National Monument. The neo-classical building, completed by Juan de Villanueva in 1785, was conceived by Charles III as a centre for the study of natural sciences. After Napoleon's troops damaged it during the Spanish Wars of Succession, it was restored by Fernando VII as a home for the royal collection of paintings and sculptures and opened as a museum in November 1819. It is unequalled in the world, with a collection numbering 7,000 pictures, of which around 1,500 are on display at any given time; there are 115 Goyas, 83 Rubens, 50 works by Velázquez, 40 Brueghels, 36 Titians, 32 El Grecos and 20 Zurbaráns. Like all great museums, the Prado is best appreciated in more than one visit. The main entrance is the Puerta de Goya, at the northern end.

Las Meninas, Las Majas and the 'dark paintings'
Do not leave the Prado without seeing Velázquez's masterpiece, *Las Meninas*, considered by many technically the finest painting in the world. Goya's *Majas* – two paintings believed to be of the Duchess of Alba, one clothed, one naked – are Madrid's own Mona Lisas for the way the spectator is invited into the picture. Goya's *pinturas negras*, are obviously the work of a man whose sanity is in decline. At once grotesque, disturbing and breathtaking, they are unique. Among them are *Saturn Devouring One of his Sons* and *Half-Drowned Dog*.

HIGHLIGHTS

- *Las Meninas*, Velázquez
- Goya's 'dark paintings'
- *The 2nd of May, The 3rd of May, Las Majas*, Goya
- *The Holy Family*, Raphael
- *The Bacchanal, Emperor Charles V in Mühlberg*, Titian
- *The Garden of Delights*, Bosch
- *The Triumph of Death*, Brueghel
- *Self Portrait*, Dürer
- *David and Goliath*, Caravaggio
- *The Three Graces*, Rubens

INFORMATION

- ⊞ dII–dIII; E9
- ✉ Paseo del Prado
- ◷ Tue–Sat 9–7; Sun 9–2
- 🍽 Bar, restaurant, café
- ☎ 91 420 36 62/420 37 68
- Ⓔ Banco de España
- 🚌 1, 2, 5, 9, 10, 14, 15, 20, 27, 34, 37, 45, 51, 52, 53, 74, 146, 150
- Ⓡ Atocha, Recoletos
- ♿ Inexpensive. Free Sat after 2:30 and free Sun
- ↔ Plaza de Cibeles (➤ 40), Museo Arqueológico Nacional (➤ 43)

Top: Goya's La Maja Desnuda

41

19

San Jerónimo el Real

HIGHLIGHTS

- Chapels
- 19th-century altar-piece by José Méndez
- 19th-century wooden pulpit
- Organ in choir, gift from Queen Maria Cristina
- Stained-glass windows
- Bronze hanging lamps

INFORMATION

- ✚ E9
- ✉ Calle Moreto 4
- ☎ 91 420 30 78
- 🕐 Daily 8–1:30, 5–6:30
- Ⓜ Banco de España, Retiro
- 🚌 10, 14, 19, 27, 34, 37, 45
- 🚆 Atocha
- 🎫 Free
- ↔ Museo del Prado (➤ 41)
- ❓ Information telephone to right of entrance
- ♿ None

This rather odd–looking church, a hybrid of architectural styles, has a certain solid power, and is breathtaking when you happen upon it during an evening stroll.

A royal church Also called Los Jerónimos, this Gothic church with a single nave and chapels between the buttresses has long been used by the Spanish monarchy as both the location for official ceremonies and as a spiritual retreat. Every prince of Asturias was sworn in here, from Philip II in 1528 to Isabella II in 1833. Alfonso XIII and Victoria of Battenberg were married here in 1906, and the present king, Juan Carlos I, was crowned here in 1975. Founded in 1464 by Henry IV as the San Jerónimo el Real Convent, on the banks of the Manzanares river, it was moved to its present site in 1503 and rebuilt for Ferdinand and Isabella. During the reign of Philip IV (1621–65), it was connected to the Casón del Buen Retiro by underground passages. The building was badly damaged during the Napoleonic Wars in 1808; during restoration carried out between 1848 and 1883, towers and pinnacles were added. This project did much to preserve the flavour of the original.

The Salón del Prado The monastery grounds once encompassed an area of Madrid set back from the Paseo del Prado between the Carrera de San Jerónimo and the Calle de Alcalá. San Jerónimo was the centrepiece of the part of the Salón known as the Huerta de los Jerónimos, or the Jerónimos Orchard. Together with the Prado of Atocha, it made up an area called the Salón del Prado, designed by José Hermosilla under instructions from Charles III between 1775 and 1782, and was in the shape of a race-track, with the two parallel avenues ending in a semicircle. The road has heavy traffic today but in the 19th century it was the great promenade of Madrid.

PALACIO DE BIBLIOTECAS Y MUSEOS

If you are interested in the ancient roots of modern Spain, the spacious, well-lit and well-organized National Library and Museum is fascinating to visit.

The building The huge Palacio de Bibliotecas y Museos, with its impressive neo-classical façade and eight-columned portico, was completed in 1892 to commemorate the 400th anniversary of the discovery of America, and is home to the Museo Arqueológico Nacional and the Biblioteca Nacional (National Library), founded by Philip III.

Archaeological Museum The museum is beautifully laid out, and the collection, covering prehistory up to (oddly for an archaeological museum) the 19th century, is as valuable artistically as it is archaeologically. Its chief attractions, dating from the period of Spain's colonisation, are the Iberian Dama de Elche and the Visigothic votive Guarrazar Crowns. The museum's entrance is at the rear of the building on Calle Serrano. Under the garden, there is a peculiar reproduction of one of the oldest cave paintings in Europe, the depiction of a herd of bison, found at Altamira.

Library On the approach to the building there are statues of Alfonso X the Wise, Cervantes and other well-known historical and literary figures. Inside, the library houses 3 million volumes and 120,000 are added every year. Particularly outstanding is the 22,000-strong collection of the texts that have shaped Spanish literary history, including a 14th-century manuscript of El Cid. None of these books are on display but temporary exhibitions of books are held.

Top: the Archaeological Museum
Right: the LIbrary

HIGHLIGHTS

- Amenemhat sarcophagus (Room 13)
- Dama de Ibiza (Room 19)
- Dama de Elche (Room 20)
- Sculpture of Livia (Room 21)
- Sundial (Room 23)
- The Guarrazar Crowns (Room 29)
- Alaferia Arches (Room 30)

INFORMATION

- E8
- Serrano 13
- 91 577 79 12
- Tue–Sat 9:30–8:30; Sun and public hols 9:30–2:30
- Serrano, Colón
- 5, 14, 21, 27, 37, 45, 53
- Recoletos
- Inexpensive. Free Sat afternoon and Sun
- Jardines del Descubrimiento (► 44)
- None

JARDINES DEL DESCUBRIMIENTO

HIGHLIGHTS

- Statue of Christopher Columbus
- Tableaux set in base of statue
- Water curtain
- Inscriptions on statues
- Skateboarders
- City Cultural Centre
- Map on wall of Cultural Centre
- Botero statues

INFORMATION

- E8
- Plaza de Colón
- Cafeteria Restaurante del Centro Cultural
- Colón
- 1, 5, 9, 14, 19, 21, 27, 37, 45, 51, 53, 74, 89
- Recoletos
- Archaeological Museum (➤ 43)

Though not particularly beautiful, the Discovery Gardens exemplify recent architectural development in Madrid and put a slice of Spanish history in concrete form.

1970s Madrid Typical of Madrid town-planning of the 1970s, these gardens in the Plaza de Colón were built to celebrate Spain's role in the discovery of the New World. The gardens are dominated by an 1892 Jerónimo Suñol statue of Christopher Columbus which faces west towards the Americas – a wedding gift from the Spanish nobility to Alfonso XII. Underneath the gardens is the Centro Cultural de la Villa de Madrid, offering theatre, concerts and exhibitions, protected from the chaos of the outside world by a deafening curtain of water. If you are lucky enough to see it working, you may well agree with those who call the fountain in the centre of the Plaza de Colón the most beautiful in Madrid.

The statues The Columbus statue is 17m high, on a base with four tableaux representing scenes from Columbus's life (Isabella offering him jewels, Columbus narrating the story of his grand project). But it is the wonderful Joaquín Vaquero Turcios sculptures from 1977 that dominate the garden. The decision to locate them so close to the more classical statues further along Paseo de la Castellana was controversial at the time. The three statues represent Columbus's three ships – the *Pinta*, the *Niña* and the *Santa María* – as they sail across the Atlantic in 1492 towards the fourth statue, which represents the New World. You can best appreciate the effect from the end of Lake Serrano.

Detail (top) on the Columbus statue

PUERTA DE ALCALÁ

If you are travelling from the airport by taxi to Madrid's centre this gateway is one of the first things you will see. It is perhaps the city's most powerful emblem, particularly viewed at night, when it is illuminated.

History Listed as a National Monument, the Puerta de Alcalá is one of the great symbols of Madrid together with Cibeles. Situated in the Plaza de la Independencia, along the line of the old city walls, it is perhaps the city's finest example of the neo-classical architecture that came as a reaction to previous baroque excesses. Commissioned by Charles III, who was to be responsible for so much of the city's architectural transformation, it was designed by Francisco Sabatini in 1778 as the main entrance to the Court. Five previous designs by other architects had been rejected.

Design Made up of five arches of granite and stone, the statue has ten columns similar to those by Michelangelo for the Capitol in Rome – facing east and crowned with Ionic capitals. Three central archways are flanked by two smaller ones. The lion heads in the centre of the three higher arches are the work of Robert Michel, and the cherubim, the trophies and the coat of arms that surmount the statue are by Francisco Gutiérrez. You can still see the bullet-marks from the 1921 assassination attempt on Eduardo Dato, the President of Madrid's Council of Ministers, on the north side of the statue. Luckily, a recent Madrid Town Council proposal to paint parts of the *puerta* white was rejected. Best appreciated when floodlit at night, the Puerta de Alcalá stands at the centre of an immense traffic junction, so it can be admired only from a distance.

DID YOU KNOW?

- A bullring stood near the site until 1873
- The Puerta is 22m high (not including shield)
- Middle arches are 10m high
- Subject of a pop song by Ana Belén

INFORMATION

- ✚ E8
- ✉ Plaza de la Independencia
- 🚇 Retiro
- 🚌 9, 19, 15, 20, 28, 51, 52, 74
- 🚉 Recoletos
- ↔ Plaza de la Cibeles (➤ 40)

PARQUE DEL RETIRO

HIGHLIGHTS

- Palacio de Cristál
- Artichoke Fountain in the Rose Garden
- Cecilia Rodriguez Gardens
- Velázquez Palace
- Statue of Alfonso XII
- Lake
- *Fallen Angel* statue
- 400-year-old cypress tree near Philip IV entrance
- Philip IV parterre
- Observatory (1790)

INFORMATION

- E9–F9–F10
- Calle Alcalá, Alfonso XII, Avenida de Menedez Pelayo, Paseo de la Reina Cristina.
- *Terrazas*
- Retiro, Atocha, Ibiza
- 2, 14, 19, 20, 26, 28, 68, 69
- Atocha
- Colección Thyssen-Bornemisza (➤ 37), Museo del Prado (➤ 41), Puerta de Alcalá (➤ 45)

Small enough that you can feel at home here and large enough to get pleasantly lost in, the Retiro park is sure to linger in your memory, particularly if you see it in late spring or early autumn when its colours are most vivid.

History The best time to visit the Retiro (retreat), a 1.2sq km space in the heart of the city, is on a sunny Sunday afternoon, when everyone in the city seems drawn to it as if by instinct. Originally thickly wooded and once a hunting ground for Philip II, the Retiro was the brainchild of the Duke of Olivares, who designed it in the 1630s for Philip IV as part of the Buen Retiro Palace – a complex of royal buildings and immense formal gardens that inspired Louis XIV at Versailles and was used until the time of Carlos III, who partially opened it to the public in the 1770s. Most of the palace was destroyed during the Napoleonic Wars.

A walk in the park Enter on Calle Alfonso XII from opposite the Casón del Buen Retiro. Walk through the parterre gardens and up the steps along a broad, shady avenue to the lake. If you want to take a boat out, head left around the lake; opposite you is a statue of Alfonso XII, a popular spot to soak up the sun. Otherwise, turn right and follow the lake round; just beyond where the water ends, turn left and you will come to the Palacio de Cristál (Glass Palace), the Retiro's loveliest building, constructed of iron and glass in 1886. Continuing straight ahead brings you to La Rosaleda, the Rose Garden. From here, another left turn takes you to the statue of the Fallen Angel (the Devil), a right turn to the Cecilia Rodríguez Gardens. A left turn at the end of the gardens will bring you to the Velázquez Palace, which hosts art exhibitions.

MUSEO LÁZARO GALDIANO

There cannot be many museums like this memorable spot, which is surprisingly unfamiliar to many madrileños. *It's a remarkable oddity, by turns tiresome and stimulating. Every time you go you discover a wonderful, new corner.*

A noble art collector José Lazaro Galdiano, an obsessive, seemingly unfocused art collector who died in 1948 at the age of 80, was born into Navarre nobility. He married Paola Florido, an Argentinian who shared his affinity for art, and together they devoted their lives to travelling the world in search of treasures. An essentially private man, Galdiano never revealed how much he paid for any of the masterpieces. On his death, he donated his collection to the state, and the museum opened its doors to the public in 1951. Despite its unevenness, it surely comprises one of the world's greatest private collections, with 30 rooms of work by Hieronymus Bosch, Bartolomé Murillo, Rembrandt, Francisco Zurbarán, El Greco, Velázquez, José de Ribera, Turner and Goya, as well as exquisite gold and silverwork, Russian enamelwork, jewellery, fans, rock crystal and weaponry.

Pleasure and pain The three-storey building that houses the collection, the neo-classical Parque Florido Palace, exemplifies the mansions put up by 18th-century *madrileño* aristocracy along the Paseo de la Castellana. A visit here can demand patience. The paintings hang in the often idiosyn-cratic order on which Galdiano insisted – 5,000 from the complete collection of 15,000 – many of them without explanatory labels; the only guide available is in Spanish and 300 pages long, there is nowhere to sit and there is no air-conditioning. Nonetheless this is easily the finest of Madrid's smaller art galleries.

HIGHLIGHTS

- *The Virgin of Charity,* Caravaggio (Room 11)
- *Landscape,* Gainsborough (Room 12)
- *Saint John in Patmos,* Bosch (Room 20)
- *Portrait of Saskia van Uylendorch,* Rembrandt (Room 21)
- *Luis de Góngora,* Velázquez (Room 23)
- *The Adoration of the Magi,* El Greco (Room 23)

INFORMATION

- ⊞ F6
- ✉ Serrano 122
- ☎ 91 561 60 84
- 🕐 Tue–Sun 10–2. Closed Aug
- Ⓡ República Argentina/ Nuñez de Balboa
- 🚌 12, 16, 19, 51, 89
- 💲 Inexpensive
- ♿ None

Top: The Adoration of the Magi *by El Greco*

Below: the Parque Florido Palace

PLAZA DE TOROS

DID YOU KNOW?

- Holds 22,000 people
- Papal bull in museum (1567) banning bullfighting
- *Portrait of Joaquín de Rodrigo*, attributed to Goya
- First fights held here in 1931
- A 'suit of lights' may contain 5kg of gold embroidery

INFORMATION

- H7
- ✉ Avenida de los Toreros, Calle Alcalá 237
- ☎ 91 725 18 57
- ⏱ Museo Taurino Tue–Fri 9:30–2:30, Sun 10–1
- Ⓜ Ventas
- 🚌 12, 21, 38, 106, 110, 146.
- Museo Taurino free
- ❓ Best visited in May during Feria de San Isidro
- ♿ None

Is bullfighting art or blood sport? No matter what your feelings, you cannot help but be impressed by the world's most important bullring, the place in which a bullfighter must triumph if he is to achieve international recognition.

History and architecture Officially opened in 1934, this is also Madrid's finest example of neo-Mudéjar architecture, a style that resurfaced during the 19th century in imitation of the Mudéjar architecture of the 13th and 14th centuries, defined by an interesting use of brickwork and attractive bright, ceramic tile inlay. In the square in front of the bullring is a melodramatically posed statue in memory of bullfighter José Cubero, inscribed with the deathless words 'a bullfighter died, and an angel was born'.

Museo Taurino Half an hour in the stuffy Museo Taurino next to the stables gives you a basic overview of the famous names in bullfighting, if not of the complex art of bullfighting itself. Massive heads of legendary bulls and portraits of great bullfighters line the walls, and there are several dramatic portrayals of bull-runs, including a notable one by artist and sculptor Mariano Benlliure (1868–1947). The highlights are the *trajes de luce* (suits of lights), as they are known, among them one belonging to Juanita Cruz, an early 20th-century woman bullfighter who was never allowed to fight on Spanish soil, and another worn by Manolete, who

Bull fight poster

perhaps the greatest of them all when he died in 1947. The museum displays are labelled both in Spanish and English, unusual in Madrid's museums.

MADRID's *best*

MUSEUMS & GALLERIES

Some tips

Museo in Spanish is not the same as 'museum' in English, but means both 'museum' and 'non-commercial art gallery' — hence the 'Museo del Prado'. Madrid has many, some unknown even to locals. Some are run by the state and others privately; the latter generally have better facilities and staff, although very few have facilities for non-Spanish speakers.

MUSEO DE ANTROPOLOGÍA

Also called the Ethnological Museum, this four-storey building was Spain's first museum of its kind. Although not comprehensive, it contains some fascinating material, exhibited in galleries devoted to different geographical areas. Of special interest are the skeleton of a 2.28m man from Badajoz, the Zairean masks and the shrunken heads from the Amazon. There is also an elegant Inuit anorak made from seal intestines.

➕ E10 ✉ Calle Alfonso XII 68 ☎ 91 530 64 18 🕐 Tue–Sat 10–7:30; Sun, public hols 10–2 🚇 Atocha, Atocha RENFE 🚌 10, 14, 27, 34, 37, 45 💷 Inexpensive 🚻 None

CASÓN DEL BUEN RETIRO

This was originally the ballroom of the Buen Retiro Royal Palace, a building destroyed by Napoleonic troops but then rebuilt by Charles III, who instructed Luca Giordano to decorate the vault with frescos. Today it contains the Prado's 19th-century Spanish art collection. A Prado ticket gets you in.

➕ E9 ✉ Calle Alfonso XII 68 ☎ 91 420 26 28/420 06 70 🕐 Tue–Sat 9–7; Sun 9–2 🍴 Restaurant 🚇 Retiro 🚌 19 💷 Inexpensive; free on Sat and Sun afternoon 🚻 Very good

Fresco in the Casón del Buen Retiro

FUNDACÍON JUAN MARCH

One of Europe's most important private art foundations, this is home to around 30 major annual exhibitions. Often among the most interesting to be found in Madrid, these have focused on Picasso, Kandinsky and Matisse. The permanent collection is largely made up of contemporary Spanish art.

➕ F7 ✉ Calle Castelló 77/Calle Padilla 36 ☎ 91 435 42 40 🕐 Mon–Sat 10–2, 5:30–9; Sun and public hols 10–2. Closed Aug and between exhibitions 🚇 Nuñez de Balboa 🚌 29, 52 💷 Free 🚻 Very good

MUSEO DE LA CIUDAD

Opened in 1992, this spacious four-storey Museum of the City is a hi-tech equivalent of the Museo Municipal, and at every step there is the odd sense of seeing Madrid repeating itself in miniature. The museum explains in almost numbing detail the workings of Madrid's transport, telephone and water systems, and there are some attractive scale models and lots of interactive displays. There are often good temporary exhibitions.

✚ F6 ⊠ Calle Principe de Vergara 140 ☎ 91 588 65 77 🕓 Tue–Fri 10–2, 4–6; Sat–Sun 10–2 📷 Cruz del Rayo 🚌 29, 52 💵 Free ❓ Guided tours can be arranged in advance ♿ Excellent

MUSEO MUNICIPAL

Built between 1721 and 1729 on the site of an old hospice, the Municipal Museum traces the history of Madrid through archaeological discoveries, paintings and maps; some lovely landscape paintings show an older, greener city, and there are works by Francisco Bayeu, Vincente Carducho and Goya – a dramatic allegory of Madrid amongst others – as well as a striking model of the city constructed in 1830. The fine baroque doorway is by Pedro Ribera, the outstanding architect of Madrid's Golden Age.

✚ d8 ⊠ Calle Fuencarral 78 ☎ 91 588 86 72 🕓 Tue–Fri 9:30–8; Sat–Sun 10–2. Closed public hols 📷 Tribunal 🚌 149 💵 Inexpensive; free on Wed and Sun ♿ None

MUSEO DE CIENCIAS NATURALES

Built in 1881, this is one of Madrid's first buildings to use glass and metal on a grand scale. In the modern section – on the left as you face it – a circular room displays hunting trophies and stuffed animals which are not for the faint-hearted, and there are a variety of audio-visuals. The museum's prize piece in the older section – *Megatherium americanum*, brought back from Argentina in 1788, was the first extinct animal ever to be scientifically classified.

✚ E6 ⊠ José Gutiérrez Abascal 2 ☎ 91 411 13 28 🕓 Tue–Fri 10–6; Sat 10–8; Sun and public hols 10–2 📷 Nuevos Ministerios 🚌 14, 27, 40, 147, 150 💵 Inexpensive ♿ Few; steps to entrance

MUSEO ROMÁNTICO

This monument to faded romantic glory founded in 1924 and in urgent need of restoration, is inside a typical mid-18th-century *madrileño* building that was the home of the traveller-painter, the Marqués de Véga-Inclán. Though the content – primarily 18th-century art – might be too sentimental for some tastes, there are many items of interest, particularly Alenza's miniature *Satires of Romantic Suicide*, Goya's *Saint Gregory the Great* and a collection of Isabelline and Imperial furniture.

✚ E8 ⊠ Calle San Mateo 13 ☎ 91 448 10 45 🕓 Tue–Sat 9–3; Sun and public hols 10–2. Closed Aug 📷 Tribunal 🚌 21, 37 💵 Inexpensive; free on Sunday ♿ Very good

Closures

It is unlikely that all the sections of all the museums in Madrid have ever been open simultaneously. Redecoration and renovation, necessary evils, can be frustrating, especially since any enquiry about reopening time is likely to be met by a shrug of the shoulders. Many museums are closed on Monday.

Outside the Casón del Buen Retiro

PLAZAS

Places of celebration

Whether round or oblong the plaza, or square, is central to a Spaniard's conception of his environment. The plazas have always been focal points where the community gathers, particularly to celebrate; they still have that function today. Check at metro stations for advertisements of any events due to take place in a nearby plaza. Even if you might not understand what is going on, the lively atmosphere will reward your efforts.

PLAZA DOS DE CASCORRO

In the heart of the *barrio popular* of old Madrid, this plaza is at the top end of the fabled Rastro street market, named after the traces of blood left by animals on their way to the slaughterhouse which once stood near by – *Rastro* means 'trace'. It is a perfect place to experience the hustle and bustle of the Old Quarter on a late Sunday morning. On the right stands Los Caracoles, a long-standing seafood bar which is typical of the area. Just down Calle Ribera de Curtidores, there is a statue of local hero Eloy Gonzalo, while at the top of Calle Embajadores there is an immense mural depicting the Rastro as it was over 100 years ago.

➕ bIII; D9 ⊠ Plaza de Cascorro 🚇 La Latina, Tirso de Molina 🚌 17, 23, 35

PLAZA DE LA CEBADA

This is one of the more authentic squares even though it no longer looks like a square. Its market, opened 1875, was Madrid's first example of iron architecture; before its erection, bullfights were held on the site, and at the beginning of the 19th century, it was the scene of public executions.

➕ bIII; D9 ⊠ Plaza de Cascorro 🚇 La Latina, Tirso de Molina 🚌 17, 23, 35

PLAZA DE LAS CORTES

This is the home of the Congreso de los Diputados, or parliament buildings. The ceremonial entrance to the parliament is guarded by two bronze lions popularly known as Daoíz and Velarde after the heroic captains of the Napoleonic invasion, cast from cannons brought back from the African War in 1860. An attempted military *coup* took place inside the building in 1981, and was recorded on video for posterity. There are weekly guided tours.

➕ dIII; E9 ⊠ Plaza de las Cortes 🚇 Sevilla 🚌 5, 150, N5, N6

PLAZA DE ESPAÑA

A statue of Cervantes stands at the western end of this grandiose, slightly daunting square, overlooking a rather lovable 1815 statue of his two legendary creations, Don Quixote and Sancho

Crowds gather in the city's plazas as religious processions pass by

Panza. On the edge of the square is the Edificio España, with its neo-baroque doorway, Madrid's first true skyscraper, while the 137-m Torre Madrid was a symbol of post-Civil War economic recovery, and was Europe's tallest building when it was built in 1957.
✚ C8 ✉ Plaza de España Ⓜ Plaza de España 🚌 68, 69, 74, 133

PLAZA DE LA LEALTAD
A stone's throw from the Prado, dominated by the Ritz Hotel, this elegant, semicircular plaza is centred on an obelisk to the memory of those who died at the hands of Napoleonic troops on 3 May 1808. Their ashes are kept in an urn at the base of the monument. The Madrid Stock Exchange was built here in 1884, on a neo-classical design that neatly echoes the Prado.
✚ dII; E9 ✉ Plaza de la Lealtad Ⓜ Banco de España 🚌 10, 14, 27, 34, 37, 45

PLAZA DOS DE MAYO
This is the heart of the historic *barrio* of Malasaña, which is known as being slightly run-down and disreputable, though renovation may change that. The eponymous Manuela Malasaña and her daughter became heroes when helping to defend the area from attack during the invasion of Napoleonic troops on 2 May 1808. In the square there is a statue of the two captains who led the resistance, Daoíz and Velarde.
✚ D8 ✉ Plaza 2 de Mayo Ⓜ Bilbao 🚌 21, 147

The statue of Cervantes in the Plaza de España

PLAZA DE LA PAJA
During Muslim rule, this pleasant little square (Straw Square) was the site of the city's most important *zoco*, or street market; during the Middle Ages it housed aristocratic residences. Of the many palaces located here, the most notable is at No. 14, the Lasso de Castilla, the preferred residence of Catholic kings when they stayed in Madrid, but it is now extremely unpalatial in appearance.
✚ aIII; C9–D9 ✉ Plaza de la Paja Ⓜ La Latina 🚌 3, 31, 148

PLAZA DE SANTA ANA
Once occupied by the Santa Ana monastery, which was torn down during Joseph Bonaparte's rule (1808–13), the plaza is surrounded by bars today and is a perfect place for people-watching in summer. A statue of playwright Calderón de la Barca stands in the centre, and the Teatro Español was built in 1849 at the eastern end after the original building, an open-air theatre, was gutted by fire.
✚ cII; D9 ✉ Plaza de Santa Ana Ⓜ Sol, Sevilla 🚌 5, 150

Executions in the Plaza de la Cebada
Public executions took place in Madrid until early in this century. The instrument of death was the particularly nasty *garrote vil*, which was screwed around the neck and tightened. Most famous among the many criminals executed in the Plaza de la Cebada was Luis Candelas, the popular bandit, whose life ended in 1837.

CHURCHES

The bell of San Pedro el Viejo

'St Peter's the Elder' is so called to distinguish it from another St Peter's in Madrid of more recent construction. According to legend, the original bell was so large that it could not be taken up to the bell tower, and was left leaning against the walls overnight. The following morning it had mysteriously raised itself into the tower. The miracle led to the belief that the bell had magical powers, such as the ability to ward off thunderstorms. The bell was removed in 1565.

See Top 25 Sights for
CATEDRAL LA ALMUDENA (► 28)
CONVENTO DE LAS DESCALZAS REALES
   (► 34)
ERMITA DE SAN ANTONIO (► 24)
MONASTERIO DE LA ENCARNACIÓN (► 31)
SAN JERÓNIMO EL REAL (► 42)

CONVENTO DE SAN ANTÓN

Designed by Pedro Ribera and built by Juan de Villanueva, this example of baroque architecture houses a magnificent art collection, highlighted by Goya's *The Last Communion of Saint José de Calasanz*, painted between 1775 and 1780, and architect Ventura Rodríguez's *Dolphins* statue.

➕ E8 ✉ Hortaleza 63 ☎ 91 521 74 73 🚇 Tribunal, Chueca

SAN ANDRÉS

The undoubted highlight of this National Monument is the Capilla del Obispo (Bishop's Chapel) built between 1520 and 1530 and reflecting the transition between the Gothic and Renaissance periods. The nave and apse have Gothic vaulted ceilings, while the decorative aspects are Renaissance. The particularly fine wooden altar-piece was carved by Francisco Giralta, the paintings above it by Villoldo el Mozo. The dome over the sanctuary of the San Andrés Chapel dates from the late 15th century.

➕ alII; C9 ✉ Plaza de San Andrés 1 ☎ 91 365 48 71
🕐 Mon–Sat 8–12:30; do not visit during Mass. Closed public hols
🚇 La Latina, Tirso de Molina 🚌 3, 148 ♿ None

SAN FRANCISCO EL GRANDE

Built between 1761 and 1784, this church has a neo-classical façade by Francisco Sabatini, one of the greatest practioners of this style, and an overwhelming 33-m dome by Miguel Fernández. The monastery was used as a barracks from 1835, after which it was lavishly redecorated. The interior contains much work by Spanish masters, including an early Goya, *The Sermon of San Bernadino de Siena*, in the first chapel on the left. There is also a museum.

➕ alII; C9 ✉ Plaza de San Francisco ☎ 91 365 38 00 🕐 Tue–Sat 11–1, 4–6:30 🚇 La Latina, Tirso de Molina 🚌 3, 7, 60, 148 ♿ None

Santa Bárbara, in Calle Bárbara de Braganza

SAN ISIDRO

San Isidro is the patron saint of Madrid, and between 1885 and 1993, until the completion of the Almudena, this immense baroque church

was Madrid's unofficial cathedral. Built in 1620 by Pedro Sánchez for the Jesuits, the church was commandeered by Charles III after he expelled them. San Isidro's remains, until then in San Andrés, were brought here at that time. There is a festival in his name every May (► 22).

🕂 bIII; D9 🖂 Calle Toledo 37–39 ☎ 91 369 20 37 🚇 La Latina
🚌 17, 23, 35 ♿ None

The basilica of San Francisco el Grande

SAN NICOLÁS DE LOS SERVITAS

This is Madrid's oldest church, and though much restored after the Civil War, its tower is one of the very few echoes of the Arabic Madrid in the city. Designated as a National Monument, the tower is probably the minaret of a mosque which was later consecrated as a Catholic church. This 12th-century tower is Mudéjar (built by Moslems under Christian rule), while the central apse is Gothic. Juan de Herrera, employed by Philip II as the architect of El Escorial, was buried in the crypt in 1597.

🕂 aIII; C9 🖂 Plaza de San Nicolás 6 ☎ 91 559 40 64 🕐 Mon 9–1.30. Do not visit during Mass. Not always open; advance phone call advisable 🚇 Opera, Sol ♿ None

SAN PEDRO EL VIEJO

Noteworthy principally for its 14th-century Mudéjar tower and the legends surrounding it, San Pedro stands on the site of an old mosque. In the doorway are the only coats of arms extant from the period preceding the Catholic monarchs. Part of the interior dates from the 15th century, while the rest is largely of 18th-century construction.

🕂 aIII–bIII; D9 🖂 Calle Nuncio 14 ☎ 91 365 12 84 🕐 8–12:30, 5–8; all day Fri. Do not visit during Mass 🚇 La Latina, Tirso de Molina ♿ None

SANTA BÁRBARA (LAS SALESAS REALES)

Probably the grandest, if not the most attractive, of Madrid's churches, Las Salesas was commissioned by Bárbara de Braganza, the wife of Fernando VI. It has an elaborate façade built between 1750 and 1758 by Carlier and Moradillo, and contains Sabatini's tomb of Fernando VI (1713–59). It is currently the home of the Palacio de Justicia, or Supreme Court.

🕂 E8 🖂 Calle Bárbara de Braganza 3 🚇 Alonso Martínez, Colón

Visiting churches

When visiting churches, the normal rules apply: dress formally, wear long trousers or skirts of a decorous length and not shorts and cover your shoulders. Photos should be taken without flash, and if there is a service in progress, simply stand at the back and observe in silence. Some churches do not like visits during Mass, unless for religious purposes.

MONUMENTS & STATUES

> **See Top 25 Sights for**
> **JARDINES DEL DESCUBRIMIENTO (➤ 44)**
> **PUERTA DE ALCALÁ (➤ 45)**

Madrid's gateways

The *puertas*, or gateways of Madrid are one of its distinguishing features. Each of them was built to mark the end of one of the principal routes into the city. The Puerto de Toledo, the gateway to the city from the royal road from Andalucia, was begun by Joseph Bonaparte in 1813 and completed in 1827. It was to be the last of Madrid's gateways. They are at their best at night, when they are illuminated.

Botero's Hand *in the Castellana*

56

BOTERO STATUES
In 1994, a section of Castellana was devoted to an exhibition of sculptures by 20th-century sculptor, Fernando Botero. When the exhibition ended, *madrileños* retained a *Hand* in the middle of Castellana; the *Reclining Woman* in Calle Génova; and *Man on a Mule* in the Plaza de Colón.
➕ E8; E6 ✉ Colón. Plaza de San Juan de la Cruz 🚇 Colón. Nuevos Ministerios 🚌 7, 14, 27, 40, 147, 150

FALLEN ANGEL (RETIRO PARK)
The fallen angel in question is Lucifer: *madrileños* tell you that this is the world's only statue created in his honour. It is by Ricardo Bellver and dates from 1881.
➕ F9 ✉ Retiro. Glorieta del Angel Caido 🚇 Atocha 🚌 19, 20

FUENTE DE LOS DELFINOS
Housed in the San Antón convent on Calle Hortaleza, the *Dolphins* statue is the work of Ventura Rodríguez.
➕ E8 ✉ Calle Hortaleza 63 ☎ 91 521 74 73 🚇 Tribunal, Chueca 🚌 3, 7 ♿ None

FUENTE DE LA FAMA
The Ribera Gardens are now a playground behind the Municipal Museum; the pretty baroque fountain (Fountain of Fame) by Pedro Ribera remains a delight.
➕ D8 ✉ Jardines del Arquitecto Ribera, Calle Barceló 🚇 Tribunal 🚌 21, 37, 40, 48

FUENTE DE NEPTUNO
In the Plaza de Cánovas de Castillo, the Neptune fountain by the 18th-century sculptor Ventura Rodríguez shows the King of the Sea riding a carriage in the shape of a shell, pulled by two horses.
➕ dII; E9 ✉ Plaza de Cánovas del Castillo 🚇 Banco de España 🚌 10, 14, 27, 34, 37, 45

MUSEO DEL ARTE CONTEMPORÁNEO AL AIRE LIBRE
Connecting the Calles Juan Bravo and Eduardo Dato is a walkway over the Paseo de la Castellana. Underneath is an open-air display of sculpture by many of Spain's best-known contemporary artists.
➕ E7–F7 ✉ Paseo de la Castellana 🚇 Rubén Darío 🚌 5, 14, 27, 37, 45

PARKS & GREEN SPACES

See Top 25 Sights for
PARQUE DEL OESTE (➤ 25)
PARQUE DEL RETIRO (➤ 46)

JARDÍN BOTÁNICO

These peaceful gardens are the result of overseas expeditions in search of interesting species dating back to the 18th century. The plants and trees are carefully classified and laid out along geometrical walkways.

🞤 E9 ⊠ Plaza de Murillo 2 🚇 Atocha 🚌 10, 14, 27, 34, 37, 45

CASA DE CAMPO

In 1,723-ha Casa de Campo it is possible to walk for a couple of hours without being interrupted. The park contains sports facilities, a large lake, and the Parque de Atracciones (➤ 58) with more than 40 amusement rides from gentle merry-go-rounds to the stomach-churning Top Spin. A *teleférico* (cable car) runs up to the Parque del Oeste (➤ 25), considered to be one of the city's most delightful green spaces.

🞤 B8–B9 ⊠ Calle Marqués de Monistrol, Avenida de Portugal
🚇 Lago, Batán 🚌 41, 33, 39, 65, 75, 84

FUENTE DEL BERRO

This intricate little 17th-century garden, just south of the bullring and unfortunately close to the M30 motorway, is a well-kept secret. The attractive Berro fountain is a little piece of jungle in Madrid. There is plenty of shade in summer and several eye-catching statues.

🞤 H8 ⊠ Alcalde Sainz de Baranda 🚇 O'Donnell 🚌 15

LOS CAPRICHOS DE ALAMEDA DE OSUNA

This is the closest Madrid comes to a formal English garden. Though a fair distance from the centre, it is pleasant for Sunday strolls.

🞤 Off map ⊠ Avenida de la Alameda de Osuna 🚇 Canillejas

JARDINES DE LAS VISTILLAS

The best place in Madrid for sunset-watching, this park has wonderful views over the Casa de Campo towards the Guadarrama mountains. From late spring to autumn it's also a lively place to go in the evening for a drink.

🞤 C9–C9 ⊠ Travesía Vistillas 🚇 Opera,. La Latina 🚌 3, 148

A green city

That Madrid is Europe's greenest capital is mainly because of the 1,723-ha Casa de Campo, 'the lungs of Madrid', stretching away to the northwest. Once a royal hunting estate it was opened to the public in 1931. Boats can be hired and it is considered one of the city's most attractive open spaces, a cool haven in Madrid's hot summer.

View of the city from Casa de Campo

ATTRACTIONS FOR CHILDREN

See Top 25 Sights for
PARQUE DEL OESTE (► 25)
PARQUE DEL RETIRO (► 46)

Tren de la Fresa

Hostesses in costume serve strawberries to passengers on this old steam train, which is called the Strawberry Train because it runs between Madrid and the Aranjuez strawberry fields. A hundred years ago the trip was a favourite weekend jaunt for *madrileños*. Tickets can be booked from many travel agents, and include entrance to the Royal Palace and gardens in Aranjuez.

ACCIONA

Acciona, Madrid's first interactive science museum is full of hands-on exhibits that teach children that science can be fun. Unfortunately, Sailing through Images and A World of Molecules, among other sections, are all in Spanish. The museum is a 15-minute bus ride from the city centre.
🔹 Off map 🖂 Pintor Murillo. Parque de Andalucía, Alcobendas ☎ 91 661 39 09 🕐 Mon–Fri 10–6; Sat, Sun and public hols 10–8 🚇 Plaza Castilla (for bus departures) 🚌 Plaza Castilla (every 20 minutes)

AQUÓPOLIS

Spanish children beg their parents to take them to Aquópolis, the biggest and best of the Madrid water parks and one of the largest in Europe. There are huge water slides, an adventure lake and wave machines.
🔹 Off map 🖂 Villanueva de la Cañada. Carretera de El Escorial 25km ☎ 91 815 69 11 🕐 Mon–Fri 12–8; Sat, Sun and public hols 11–8 🍴 Cafés

FARO DE MONCLOA

This 92m-stainless steel tower, opposite the entrance to the Museo de América, was built in 1992. It offers a panoramic view of Madrid. Closed in bad weather.
🔹 C7 🖂 Avenida de la Victoria ☎ 91 544 81 04 🕐 Daily 10:30–2:15, 4:30–7:15 (8:15 in summer) 🚇 Moncloa 🚌 16, 61, 83, 84, 92, 93, 95 🎟 Inexpensive

PARQUE DE ATRACCIONES (CASA DE CAMPO)

This enormous fun-fair offers everything from merry-go-rounds to the breathtaking Tornado roller coaster, plus open-air concerts in summer.
🔹 A9 🖂 Casa de Campo ☎ 91 463 29 00 🕐 Mon–Fri noon–1AM; Sat and public hols noon–2AM 🍴 Cafés, restaurants 🚇 Batán 🚌 33, 36, 39, 65 🎟 Moderate

ZOO

Madrid's zoo in the Casa de Campo is one of the best in Europe. It contains over 2,000 animals and more than 100 species of bird, including 29 endangered species. There is a dolphinarium with twice-daily shows, a train ride, an aquarium and a special children's section. Parrot shows, the tank of sharks and birds of prey are very popular.
🔹 A9 🖂 Casa de Campo ☎ 91 711 99 50 🕐 Daily 10:30–9:30 🍴 Cafés, restaurants 🚇 Batán 🚌 33, Ventas – Zoo, Batán – Zoo, Estrecho – Zoo, Peñaprieta – Zoo 🎟 Expensive

The dolphinarium – a perennial attraction at the zoo in the Casa de Campo

INTERESTING STREETS

ARENAL
Connecting Sol with Opera, the Calle Arenal has a 19th-century air. During the Middle Ages it was no more than a ravine, but after 1656 it began to compete with the Calle Mayor in importance, perhaps because it was the shortest route between the Royal Palace and Sol. Highlights are the San Ginés Church and the Joy Esclava discotheque.
➕ bII; D9 ⬛ Sol, Opera 🚌 5, 15, 20, 51, 52, 53, 150

GRAN VÍA
Running between the Calle Alcalá and the Plaza de España, the imposingly massive Gran Vía is one of the city's great axes; with its shops and cinemas it is very lively and stimulating for early evening strolls. Begun in 1910 under Alfonso XII, it led to the shortening or destruction of 54 other streets. Highlights are the Grassy Reloj and Telefónica buildings.
➕ bI–cI–dI ⬛ E8 ⬛ Gran Vía, Callao 🚌 44, 46, 74, 133, 146, 147, 148, 149

MAYOR
This is perhaps the most traditional of Madrid's streets, with some pokey, old-fashioned shops – including a rather wonderful *guitarrería* (guitar shop) near the Calle Bailén end. Spain's two greatest playwrights, Lope de Vega and Calderón de la Barca, lived at Nos. 25 and 61 respectively.
➕ all–bII; D9 ⬛ Sol 🚌 3

MESÓN DE PAREDES
To get a complete sense of the slightly surreal and multicultural atmosphere of Madrid's *barrio popular*, stroll down this street and those around it on any weekday morning when it is bustling and full of life. La Corrala is an 1882 example of the corridor-tenement found throughout working class Madrid and from the early 1980s used for productions as an open-air theatre. It is now an Artistic Monument.
➕ bIII–cIII–cIV; D9–D10 ⬛ Tirso de Molina, Lavapiés 🚌 32, 57

PASEO DE LA CASTELLANA
Running in an almost straight line from Colón for 6km to Plaza de Castilla, the Castellana is one of Madrid's main points of reference. It splits the city in two, and many major sights are located on or around it.
➕ E2–E8 ⬛ Colón, Rubén Darío, Nuevos Ministerios, Lima, Cuzco, Plaza de Castilla 🚌 5, 14, 27, 40, 45, 147, 149, 150

Streets and sky
Madrileños live on the streets, particularly during the summer, so a description of any one of them is also a portrait of the people who work and live there. Look for the old ladies selling lottery tickets lined up on their seats in the Plaza del Sol, the waiters in the Plaza Mayor and the market traders in the Retiro. Remember to look upwards, too: on clear days, the contrast between the buildings and the blue sky is exhilarating.

The Gran Vía, one of Madrid's major streets

CURIOSITIES

MURALLA ARABE

What little we can see of the Arab Wall is the oldest surviving part of Madrid. It was originally part of the walls of the small Arab town of Magerit. The area around it, now the Parque Emir Mohammed I, is one of the venues for Madrid's autumn arts festival (➤ 22).

➕ all; C9 ✉ Cuesta de la Vega 🚇 Opera 🚌 3, 41, 148

ESTACIÓN DE ATOCHA

Some 2000sq m of indoor tropical garden can be found inside this impressive late 18th-century

wrought iron structure by Alberto del Palacio.

➕ dIV; E10 ✉ Plaza del Emperador Carlos V ☎ 91 527 31 60 🚇 Atocha 🚌 14, 27, 34, 37, 45 ♿ Few

Façade of the Atocha Railway Station

CASA DE LAS SIETE CHIMENEAS

Legend has it that Philip II built the House of the Seven Chimneys in the 1580s for one of his mistresses, who is supposed to haunt the house. When restoration work was done, the skeleton of a woman was discovered with coins from the period of Philip II nearby.

➕ dI, E8 ✉ Plaza del Rey 🚇 Banco de España 🚌 1, 2, 74, 146

SALA DEL CANAL DE ISABEL II

Considered one of Madrid's finest examples of industrial architecture, this display space, built in neo-Mudéjar style between 1907 and 1911, mounts frequent excellent photographic exhibitions.

➕ D6 ✉ Calle Santa Engracia 125 ☎ 91 445 10 00 🕐 Tue–Sat 10–2, 5–9; Sun and public hols 10–2 🚇 Cuatro Caminos 🚌 3, 37, 149 💷 Free

TORRES KIO (PUERTA DE EUROPA)

These towers are named after the Kuwaiti Investment Office, which withdrew funding half-way through construction. The walls are angled inwards at 15 degrees – more than that and they would collapse.

➕ E3 ✉ Plaza de Castilla 🚇 Plaza de Castilla 🚌 5, 27, 42, 124, 125, 147, 149

VIADUCT

Known as 'the Suicide Bridge' until the council put up suicide-proof screens in 1997. These have taken away from the drama of the views as you gaze down on the Calle de Segona far below.

➕ C9 ✉ Calle Bailén 🚇 Opera 🚌 3, 148

Curious facts

Behind its walls Tirso de Molina metro station has skeletons, discovered when the station was built in the 1920s. They proved to be bones from the Convent of the Merced, which previously stood on this site. Also curious is that Madrid has not been particularly careful about the remains of some of its greatest artists: the whereabouts of Velázquez, Lope de Vega and Cervantes are unknown, while the skeleton of Goya is headless.

MADRID
where to...

FINE DINING

Prices

In a luxury restaurant expect to pay over 7,500ptas per person for three courses, wine and coffee.

Tips for Dining

Many of Madrid's better restaurants are more enjoyable in the evenings than at lunchtime, when they attract a mainly business clientele. Only Zalacaín insists on a jacket and tie. Only in pricier restaurants is there a chance that the waiter will speak English. Restaurants are generally open until midnight and so serve food until 10:30–11. Some of the best restaurants are in the best hotels: Berceo-Le Divellec in the Hotel Villa Magna (☎ 91 587 12 34); Belagua in the Santo Mauro (☎ 91 369 69 00). There is no protocol about tipping: leave 5–10 per cent of the bill if you feel the meal and service deserved it.

CANDELA

This perennial favourite with politicians and other luminaries from the entertainment world serves huge chunks of Argentinian meat (prepared in view) in an atmosphere of elegant informality and spaciousness.

✚ E5 ✉ Calle Santo Domingo de Silos ☎ 91 562 79 42 🚇 Santiago Bernabeu

CLUB 31

One of Madrid's finest restaurants serves international fare including a fair amount of excellent game. Try the partridge with grapes. Formal and elegant, with impeccable service.

✚ E8 ✉ Calle Alcalá 58 ☎ 91 532 05 11 🕒 Closed Aug 🚇 Retiro

LOS CUATRO ESTACIONES

As the name Four Seasons suggests, the menu changes through the year to provide the best available ingredients. Traditional cuisine with a creative twist.

✚ D6 ✉ Calle General Ibañez de Ibero 5 ☎ 91 553 63 05 🚇 Guzmán el Bueno

LA GASTROECA DE STÉPHANE Y ARTURO

Black and pink interior and imaginative French cuisine are the hallmarks of this high-class bistro opened in 1987 by French artist Arturo Guérin and his wife.

✚ dl; E8 ✉ Plaza de Chueca 8 ☎ 91 532 25 64 🕒 Closed Aug 🚇 Chueca

HORCHER

Perhaps the best-known restaurant in Madrid after Zalacaín (see below). Established in 1943 and family-run, with exquisite menu of central European dishes and game.

✚ E9 ✉ Calle Alfonso XII 6 ☎ 91 522 07 31 🕒 Closed Aug 🚇 Retiro

PEDRO LARUMBE

Opened in 1996, this has quickly acquired classic status for the creativity of its Mediterranean cuisine. Its three salons occupy the third floor of a beautiful neo-classical building, with a delightful summertime *terraza*.

✚ F7 ✉ Calle de Serrano 61 ☎ 91 575 11 22 🕒 Closed 2 weeks in Aug 🚇 Rubén Dario

VIRIDIANA

Hung with stills from Buñuel movies. The menu is extremely creative, serving superior modern Spanish food. The atmosphere is unusually mellow.

✚ dll; E9 ✉ Calle Juan de Mena 14 ☎ 91 523 44 78 🕒 Closed Aug 🚇 Retiro

ZALACAÍN

Generally considered one of Madrid's best restaurants. The Basque/Navarre menu changes seasonally according to the whims of head chef, Benjamin Urdiain.

✚ E6 ✉ Alvarez de Baena 4 ☎ 91 561 48 40 🕒 Closed Christmas and Easter week 🚇 Rubén Dario

BUDGET DINING

ALBUR
Excellent Spanish cooking using local ingredients with a different menu of typical regional dishes every day.
✚ D7 ✉ Calle Manuela Malasaña ☎ 91 594 27 33 Ⓜ Bilbao

ARTEMISA
The best of a very few vegetarian restaurants. Green beans in a pine-nut and mayonnaise sauce is a speciality.
✚ cII; E9 ✉ Ventura de la Vega 4 ☎ 91 429 50 92 Ⓜ Sol

EL ECONÓMICO
Something of a legend among Madrid's penny-pinchers, and one of the few places that has still not broken the 1,000ptas barrier for its *menu del día*. Good basic Castilian food.
✚ cIV; D10 ✉ Calle Argumosa 9 ☎ 91 539 41 95 Ⓜ Lavapiésl

GULA GULA
Bright-coloured and centrally located. A good self-service salad bar and a nightly cabaret (in Spanish) that makes the meal memorable. There is a smaller and less frenetic branch in Calle Infante.
✚ cII; E8 ✉ Gran Via 1 ☎ 91 522 87 64 Ⓜ Sevilla

HYLOGUI
Enormous, bustling and one of the better basic Spanish food establishments, with more than 100 items on the menu and better-than-average service.

Queues at weekends.
✚ cII; E9 ✉ Calle Ventura de la Vega 3 ☎ 91 429 73 57 🕐 Closed Aug Ⓜ Sevilla

NO-DO
At the smart end of town, this airy, open-plan locale is the place to be seen. Cuisine is mouth-watering Mediterranean/Japanese fusion. The 'No-Do Box', a four dish-sampler, is recommended.
✚ F6 ✉ Calle Veláquez 50 ☎ 91 564 40 44 Ⓜ República Argentine

SALVADOR
Hosts intellectuals, bullfighters and other clients in the spirit of one of its long-ago regulars, Ernest Hemingway. Traditional food, with good oxtail and cod fritters.
✚ dI; E8 ✉ Calle Barbieri 12 ☎ 91 521 45 24 🕐 Closed Aug Ⓜ Chueca, Gran Via

SAMARKANDA
Attractive restaurant in the tropical garden section of the Atocha railway station with good light, modern, international cuisine. Ask for table No. 20.
✚ E10 ✉ Glorieta de Carlos V, Atocha Railway Station ☎ 91 530 97 46 Ⓜ Atocha

VIUDA DE VACAS
Madrileños like to bring their overseas visitors here for traditional Spanish cooking amid *azulejo* tiles and wooden tables. Excellent value.
✚ bIII; D9 ✉ Calle Cava Alta 33 ☎ 91 366 58 47 🕐 Closed Aug Ⓜ La Latina

Prices
In a budget restaurant you should be able to find a good meal for under 4,500ptas, including wine.

Budget eating
Many restaurants offer a *menu del día* (often hidden away at the back of the menu) that includes a first and second course, wine and a dessert or coffee. It is not a bad idea to eat early (around 1:30–2) if you want this menu as the best items may have gone by the time you arrive. *Paella* on Thursday, for example, is always in demand.

MADRILEÑO CUISINE

Prices per person
£ = 1,500–4,500ptas
££ = 4,500–7,500ptas
£££ = 7,500–12,000ptas

Madrid gastronomy

In Madrid cuisine, the animal parts that tend to produce a grimace of disgust play a major part: you'll find the spicy *callos a la madrileña* (offal), *orejas* (pig's ears), *sesos* (brains) and different kinds of *morcilla* (blood sausage). Perhaps the most acceptable dish to non-native palates is the classic *cocido completo*: first a noodle soup, then a main course with meat, chickpeas and other vegetables, all cooked together.

CAFÉ DE ORIENTE (££)
Built on the remains of a convent and facing the Royal Palace, this is a rather aristocratic place with distinctive dishes that creatively fuse *madrileño* with French cuisine.
⊞ all; D9 ✉ Plaza de Oriente ☎ 91 576 01 37 🚇 Ópera

CASA ALBERTO (£)
Rich in character, this restaurant founded in 1827, is at the back of a bar which serves terrific *tapas*. It's full of bullfighting memorabilia. The ham croquettes and oxtail are recommended.
⊞ cIII; D9 ✉ Calle Huertas 18 ☎ 91 429 93 56 🕐 Closed 2 weeks in Aug 🚇 Antón Martín

CASA DOMINGO (£)
Callos (tripe) is the speciality in this somewhat noisy 1920s restaurant, which spills out on to the pavement opposite the Parque del Retiro. *Tortilla de bacalao* (cod tortilla) is another unusual speciality. Wonderful home-made desserts.
⊞ F8 ✉ Calle Alcalá 99 ☎ 91 576 01 37 🚇 Retiro

CASA LUCIO (£££)
The King has been known to bring visitors to this Madrid classic; the least touristy of Madrid's traditional restaurants, Casa Lucio specialises in Castilian roasts but in addition offers several first-class Basque dishes.
⊞ alll; D9 ✉ Cava Baja 35 ☎ 91 365 32 52 🕐 Closed Aug 🚇 La Latina, Tirso de Molina

CASA MANOLO (£)
Its location close to the Congress Building means this modernised 1896 tavern attracts a high-profile political clientele. Its fin-de-siècle Madrid design are a monument to the culinary status quo.
⊞ dll; E8 ✉ Calle Jovellanos 7 ☎ 91 521 45 16 🕐 Mon–Sat. Closed Aug 🚇 Banco de España

LOS GALAYOS (££)
The best restaurant close to the Plaza Mayor, serving traditional roasts. *Terraza* for open-air dining.
⊞ bll; D9 ✉ Calle Botaneras 5 ☎ 91 366 30 28 🚇 Sol

LA GRAN TASCA (£££)
Famed for its rich and heavy but delicious *cocido madrileño* (Madrid stew). Business lunches, more laid-back dinners.
⊞ E7 ✉ Santa Engracia 22 ☎ 91 488 77 79 🕐 Mon–Sat 🚇 Alonso Martínez

MALACATÍN (££)
The city's only self service *cocido* restaurant (see panel), a peculiarity which makes it popular with the locals. It also offers a range of other good dishes. Reserve ahead.
⊞ blll; D9 ✉ Calle Ruda 5 ☎ 91 365 52 41 🕐 Mon–Sat. Closed last 2 weeeks in Jul, Aug 🚇 La Latina

BASQUE & CATALAN CUISINE

EL AMPARO (£££)
Lovingly designed with an eye for tradition with a small interior patio. Basque cuisine and a wine list with 500 choices.
F8 ⊠ Callejón de Puigcerdá 8 Libertad 16 ☎ 91 431 64 56 ⏲ Closed Aug 🚇 Serrano

CABO MAYOR (£££)
This relaxed Madrid classic in elegant nautical style, specialises in the cuisine of Cantabria in northern Spain. The lobster salad and the desserts are particularly good.
F4 ⊠ Calle Juan Ramón Jiménez 37 ☎ 91 350 87 76 ⏲ Closed Easter week and Aug 🚇 Plaza de Castilla, Cuzco

CARMENCITA (£)
This pleasant, relaxed bistro in a central location is one of the city's lower-priced Basque restaurants, also offers *madrileño* cuisine.
dl; E8 ⊠ Calle Libertad 16 ☎ 91 531 6612 ⏲ Mon–Fri, Sat dinner only 🚇 Banco de España

ENDAVANT (££)
Spacious, with a Mediterranean air and Catalan-based cuisine including snails and a delicious *crema catalana* (custard). Outdoor dining in summer.
F6 ⊠ Calle Velázquez 160 ☎ 91 561 27 38 🚇 República Argentina

ERROTA–ZAR (££)
Centrally located. Basque-style grilled meat and fish are the specialities here. In a side room, opened in

1997, you can help yourself to *txiri* Basque wine in elegant but informal surroundings.
dll; D9 ⊠ Calle Jovellanos 3 ☎ 91 531 25 64 🚇 Sevilla

LA FONDA (££)
One of the first Catalan restaurants to open in the city, offering cuisine with a creative touch, in the city's most exclusive shopping district.
F8 ⊠ Calle Lagasca ☎ 91 577 79 24 🚇 Retiro

JULIAN DE TOLOSA (£££)
In a 19th-century building you'll find a concise but stunningly prepared range of dishes; the steaks and grilled peppers stand out.
blll; D9 ⊠ Cava Baja 18 ☎ 91 365 82 10 ⏲ Mon–Sat 🚇 La Latina

OTER EPICURE (£££)
Among the Basque and Navarre offerings, the salted fish is excellent. You can sample any of 175 wines and try any of the many cigars before you buy.
F7 ⊠ Calle Claudio Coello 71 ☎ 91 431 67 70 ⏲ Mon–Sat 🚇 Nuñez de Balboa

EL PINTXO (££)
A Basque cider-house as well as a this restaurant offers traditional uncomplicated but well-prepared cuisine from the region, including a particularly mouthwatering hake *tortilla*.
F4 ⊠ Calle Victor Andrés Belaúnde 8 ☎ 91 458 65 23 🚇 Colombia

Regional cuisine

Spanish regional cuisine – particularly that of the Basque country – has achieved greater international recognition than the cuisine of Madrid itself. Basque and Catalan cuisine tends to be fish-based, though if you do order meat, it is likely to come in the form of a huge steak. Basque *tapas* are available at some of the Basque restaurants; these are little culinary works of art.

GALICIAN & ASTURIAN CUISINE

Regional fare

After the Basques, the Galicians have the best cuisine in Spain. Together with their neighbours the Asturians, they prefer maritime cuisine, and the portions will generally be sizeable and sumptuous, with potatoes the staple food. Regional specialities include *pulpo* (squid), and *pimentos de Padrón* (hot green peppers) that are generally best eaten with a large jug of water.

LA BURBUJA QUE RÍE (£)

The Laughing Bubble is aptly named: the capital's lightest-hearted, busiest Asturian restaurant, with a mainly young clientele. Look for huge pots of steaming mussels; the cheeses are worth sampling.
🔒 alll ✉ Calle Angel 16 ☎ 91 366 51 97 🚇 Puerta de Toledo

CASA GALLEGA (£)

The specials are largely Galician and fish-based but you'll also find fabulous Padrón peppers, as well as wonderful *tapas* in the basement bar. Service is friendly, if slow.
🔒 bll; D9 ✉ Plaza de San Miguel 8 ☎ 91 547 30 55 🚇 Sol

CASA D'A TROYA (££)

Worth the trip off the beaten track to a hard-to-find street. This spot is reasonably-priced, considering it offers the best Galician food in Madrid. Seafood, especially the lobster salad, is the speciality of the house.
🔒 H5 ✉ Calle Emiliano Barral 14 ☎ 91 416 44 55 🕐 Mon–Sat. Closed last 2 weeks of Jul, Aug 🚇 Avienda de la Paz

CASA PARRONDO (££)

Traditional Asturian cuisine and the steaming platefuls of *fabada* (meat and potato stew) are made with ingredients from the Parrondo family's own garden. Convenient placed in a central location.
🔒 bll; D8 ✉ Calle Trujillos 4 ☎ 91 522 62 34 🕐 Closed Aug 🚇 Santo Domingo

COMBARRO (£££)

Mouthwatering seafood brought in daily from Galicia. The buzzing ground-floor *tapas* bar is one of Madrid's most attractively laid-out.
🔒 D5 ✉ Calle Reina Mercedes 12 ☎ 91 554 77 84 🕐 Mon–Sat. Closed Aug 🚇 Alvarado

HOGAR GALLEGO (££)

A central location just off the Plaza Mayor, with outdoor seating in summer, makes this the most popular Galician restaurant with visitors.
🔒 bll; D9 ✉ Plaza Comandante Morenas 3 ☎ 91 542 48 26 🕐 Closed Aug 🚇 Sol

O'PAZO (£££)

The king of Galician cuisine in Madrid, Don Evaristo García Gómez, serves marvellous Galician fare – seafood cocktail, Aguinaga eels and a classic *tarta de Santiago* for dessert.
🔒 E5 ✉ Calle Reina Mercedes 20 ☎ 91 553 23 33 🕐 Closed Easter week and Aug 🚇 Estrecho

TERRA MUNDI (££)

Decorated like a rustic Galician farmhouse this serves good *tapas* and a variety of meat and fish dishes, of which grilled octopus stands out. The *menu del día* is reasonably-priced.
🔒 clll ✉ Lope de Vega 32 ☎ 91 429 52 80 🚇 Antón Martin

LATIN-AMERICAN CUISINE

EL CENTRO CUBANO (£)

The Cuban Centre is as much a cultural project as it is a restaurant: walls are covered with press-cuttings and photos of Cuban stars past and present. Go for *ropa vieja* (meat stew) and *arroz a la cubana* (rice with tomato sauce and a banana).

F8 ✉ Calle Claudio Coello ☎ 91 575 82 79 Ⓜ Serrano

EL CHALET (££)

Summer is the best time to visit this spot with more than 280sq m of pine-shaded lawns. One area is for families; the the other is more intimate. The Argentinian beef is the speciality.

H4 ✉ Calle Arturo Soria 207 ☎ 91 415 64 00 Ⓜ Arturo Sonia

EL CHIVITO DE ORO (£)

One of Madrid's few Uruguayan restaurants is tiny, with only eight tables. Meat based cuisine, with the *matambre* the speciality.

E7 ✉ Plaza de Chamberi 2 ☎ 91 448 78 93 Ⓜ Iglesia

ENTRE SUSPIRO Y SUSPIRO (££)

The best Mexican restaurant in Madrid is colourful, with a menu in verse. Book ahead.

bll; D9 ✉ Calle Caños del Peral 3 ☎ 91 542 06 44 Ⓜ Mon–Sat. Closed Aug Ⓜ Opera

LA HABABERA (£)

Pleasant and intimate Cuban restaurant. Ask for *mojitos* (long drink based on rum) or *daiquris* (Cuban liqueur) as you wait. Live music on Saturday nights.

bll; D9 ✉ Plaza de Herradores 10 ☎ 91 542 80 56 Ⓜ Sol

PATACÓN PISAO (£)

A rare example of a Colombian diner in Madrid, a ten-minute subway ride from the centre. Functional, but delightful atmosphere in the evenings as it fills with Colombians yearning for meat-based home cooking: *bandeja* (a kind of stew) is the house speciality.

E10 ✉ Calle Las Delicias 10 ☎ 91 467 39 95 Ⓜ Palos de la Frontera

LA TAQUERÍA (£)

An atmospheric Mexican spot. Try *tacos del pastor*, prepared in the traditional way, and the *enchiladas* – and don't miss the wonderful *margaritas*.

D8 ✉ Plaza de las Comendadoras 2 ☎ 91 522 80 49 Ⓜ Closed Aug Ⓜ Noviciado

LA VACA ARGENTINA (££)

A successful Spanish restaurant chain, serves meat that arrives vacuum-packed daily from Argentina. The meat is served raw and then cooked by you to your taste on red-hot plates.

alll; D9 ✉ Calle Bailén 20 ☎ 91 365 66 54 Ⓜ La Latina

New tastes

For historical and geographical reasons both Latin American and North African cuisine are increasingly popular on Madrid's hitherto fairly conservative culinary scene. The menus can be as incomprehensible to Spaniards as to any visitor. The best bet is to see what others are eating and order what looks appealing.

COFFEE, TEA & CHOCOLATE

La tertulia

Until not so long ago, Madrid had *tertulia* (culture devoted to literary gatherings). Writers, philosophers and artists would meet to drink coffee (and stronger brews, too), to smoke and to debate ideas, to such an extent that poet and musician Emilio Cerrère was inspried to declare that most literary masterpieces were written in cafés. The *tertulia* also gave rise to another phenomenon: the so-called *naufragos del café* (coffee shipwrecks), men who went to *tertulias* only to become lost in a world of unrealisable dreams. Nowadays the tradition has moved to TV and has a new name — the chat show.

CAFÉ COMERCIAL
'Time hasn't actually stopped in this café,' declared the newspaper *El País*, 'but it does move imperceptibly slowly'. The Comercial, calm through the day but hectic at night, has long been Madrid's best-known meeting point.
✚ D7 ✉ Glorieta de Bilbao 7 ☎ 91 521 56 55 🕒 Closed Aug 🚇 Bilbao

CAFÉ DEL BOTÁNICO
Its position next to the Prado and the Retiro makes this one of the city's better-located cafés. A *terraza* is open in summer.
✚ E9 ✉ Calle Ruiz de Alarcón 27 ☎ 91 420 23 42 🚇 Atocha, Banco de España

CAFÉ DEL NUNCIO
This friendly place in the old quarter is at its best in summer, when the *terraza* is open.
✚ allI; D9 ✉ Calle Segovia 9 ☎ 91 366 09 06 🚇 La Latina

CAFÉ DE ORIENTE
One of the more exclusive cafés with sumptuous decor and a particularly good view of the Palacio Real.
✚ all; C9 ✉ Plaza de Oriente 2 ☎ 91 547 15 64 🚇 Opera

CAFÉ GIJÓN
Best known for its literary associations, but still a pleasant place to stop.
✚ dl; E8 ✉ Paseo de Recoletos 21 ☎ 91 521 54 25 🚇 Banco de España, Colón

CAFÉ RUIZ
A relatively peaceful retreat from the night-time mayhem of the surrounding *barrio* of Malasaña, the Ruiz retains a late 19th-century feel and serves cocktails as well as coffee and milkshakes.
✚ D7 ✉ Calle Ruiz 11 ☎ 91 446 12 32 🚇 Bilbao

CAFÉ VIENA
Coffee, hot chocolate and cakes, in plush surroundings.
✚ C8 ✉ Calle Luisa Fernanda 23 ☎ 91 559 38 28 🚇 Ventura Rodriguez

CHOCOLATERÍA SAN GINÉS
Flashy, big, and extremely busy, especially in winter. Three minutes from Sol.
✚ bII; D9 ✉ Pasaje de San Ginés 5 ☎ 91 365 65 46 🚇 Sol, Opera

EMBASSY
Madrid is short on tea-rooms, but this is the best, serving a wide range of teas as well as chocolates, cakes, sandwiches and scones.
✚ E8 ✉ Paseo de la Castellana 12 ☎ 576 00 80 🚇 Colón

EL ESPEJO
With its fabulous art-nouveau decor and a terrace, El Espejo looks more expensive than it is.
✚ dl; E8 ✉ Paseo de Recoletos 31 ☎ 91 308 23 47 🚇 Colón

NUEVO CAFÉ BARBIERI
A columned interior and youthful clientele.
✚ cIV; D10 ✉ Calle Avemaría 45 ☎ 91 527 36 58 🚇 Lavapiés

TAPAS

ALOQUE
A wide range of fish and meat-based *tapas* is available in this homely, friendly-staffed locale. The food on offer changes with the seasons to ensure freshness. It is its 300-strong wine list that dominates, with 250 of them of Spanish origin. The cheese pies are worth trying.

cll; D9 ✉ Torrecilla del Leal ☎ 91 528 36 62 🕐 Closed Aug 🚇 Antón Martín

EL ANCIANO REY DE LOS VINOS
Particularly famous for its wines, this is one of the more historic taverns of Madrid, with its *azulejo* tiles. Typical Madrid *tapas* are available, including fried cod, tripe and meatballs.

cll; D9 ✉ Calle de la Paz ☎ 91 532 14 73 🕐 Closed Aug 🚇 Sol

CASA HUMANES
Casa Humanes was a favourite of King Alfonso XII. With its well-preserved turn-of-the-20th-century furnishings, it sells tiny glasses of red wine at 25ptas a shot. *Tapas* displayed.

D10 ✉ Calle Embajadores 80 🕐 Closed Aug 🚇 Embajadores

CASA LABRA
The Spanish Socialist Party was founded here in 1879 just 19 years after the bar was established, and Casa Labra has been producing typically *madrileño tapas* ever since. Cod croquettes a speciality.

cll; D9 ✉ Calle Tetuán 12 ☎ 91 531 00 81 🚇 Sol

CASA MINGO
A popular Asturian *sidrería* or cider house. The idea is to pour the cider into the glass from a great height and drink it very fast. The best *tapas* are based on the strong *Cabrales* cheese. The restaurant is excellent.

B8 ✉ Paseo de la Florida 34 ☎ 91 547 79 18 🚇 Norte

JOSÉ LUIS
Firmly non-traditional, José Luis offers international-based *tapas* such as smoked salmon tartare and melted brie.

F7 ✉ Calle de Serrano 89 ☎ 91 563 09 58 🚇 Serrano

LHARDY
One of the city's classier restaurants and a local institution. The good range of fairly pricey *tapas* include consommé, croquettes, Russian salad on bread and, in summer, Madrid's best gazpacho. *Tapas* displayed.

cll; D9 ✉ Calle Carrera de San Jerónimo 8 ☎ 91 522 22 07 🚇 Sol

TABERNA DE ANTONIO SÁNCHEZ
The best-conserved of all the *tapas* bars pays homage to the bullfighting family that has run it since 1830. Displays of bullfighting (including bulls' heads) make the distinctive setting as fascinating as the *tapas*.

bIII; D9 ✉ Calle Mesón de Paredes 13 ☎ 91 539 78 62/68 🚇 Tirso de Molina

Tapas
The *tapa*, a snack to accompany your drink, is a part of Spanish culture: it started in the 18th century when Carlos III insisted that his entourage cover their wine with a plate of food to keep dust from getting into it (*tapa* means 'lid'). Free *tapas* are largely a thing of the past, and many bars no longer display their wares, which can make it hard to order. It may be worth eating in places where the *tapas* are kept behind glass, so you can see them before buying. Pay for what you have eaten and drunk before leaving, rather than on a round-by-round basis. Many *cervecerías* (late-night bars) sell *tapas*, an atmospheric venue for a late night snack (➤ 78).

69

Markets & Shopping Streets

The municipal food markets

There are many of these around Madrid and each *barrio* has its own. All offer a vast range of foodstuffs at extremely competitive prices – and therefore loaded with atmosphere – there are shoppers in these places who would kill to save a few pesetas on a clove of garlic. Especially worth visiting: San Miguel ✉ Plaza de San Miguel, is right in the centre of town; Maravillas ✉ Bravo Murillo 122, the biggest; and Chamartín ✉ Calle Potosi, the most elegantly laid out.

CALLE ALMIRANTE
During the 1980s, the Calle Almirante became a kind of Calle de Carnaby. Although it has declined a little since then, it is still the best area Madrid has to offer away from the far less daring formality of Ortega y Gasset and Serrano.
➕ E8 ✉ Calle Almirante 🚇 Chueca

CALLE JOSÉ ORTEGA Y GASSET
Now Madrid's most exclusive street with Kenzo, Adolfo Domínguez and Giorgio Armani stores.
➕ F7–G7 ✉ Calle José Ortega y Gasset 🚇 Rubén Darío, Nuñez de Balboa

CALLE DE LOS LIBREROS
A second home for Madrid's bibliophiles for over a century. A wide range of second-hand books is available with particular emphasis on the academic.
➕ bI; D8 🚇 Santo Domingo

CALLE PRECIADOS
This pedestrianised street runs between the Plaza del Sol and the Gran Via, and contains a variety of reasonably priced chain stores, many for clothes. Its central location and keen prices make it extremely crowded at Christmas
➕ bI–cI; D8–D9 🚇 Sol

CALLE DE SERRANO
You will find Adolfo Domínguez, Loewe and GianFranco Ferré stores along its length, mixed in with good chain stores nowadays.
➕ F7; F8 ✉ Calle de Serrano 🚇 Serrano

CONDE DE BARAJAS MARKET
Painters try to sell their latest masterpieces in this pretty little square just behind the Plaza Mayor.
➕ bII; D9 ✉ Plaza del Conde de Barajas 🕐 Sunday morning 🚇 La Latina

MARQUÉS DE VIANA MARKET
Traditionally an area of handicrafts experts in the *barrio* of Tetuán.
➕ D4–E4 ✉ Calle Marqués de Viana 🕐 Sunday morning 🚇 Tetuán

RASTRO STREET MARKET
On a Sunday morning, from about 10.30 to 3, the streets around Ribera de Curtidores are alive with people buying and selling just about everything. A lot of the wares, particularly in the side streets, are junk, but the people-watching is great. Calle Ribera de Curtidores has furniture, antiques and camping shops.
➕ bIII–bIV; D9–D10 ✉ Plaza de Cascorro, Calle Ribera and sidestreets 🕐 Sunday and public hols 🚇 La Latina, Tirso de Molina

STAMPS AND COINS MARKET
People meet to discuss stamps and coins under the archways of the Plaza Mayor.
➕ bII; D9 ✉ Plaza Mayor 🕐 Sunday morning 🚇 Sol

KEY SHOPS & MALLS

ABC SERRANO
Set in a building that once housed the ABC newspaper, this elegant mall on five levels has gifts, crafts, fashion together with restaurants and cafés. Top Madrid is an attractive rooftop bar in summer.

➕ F7 ✉ Calle de Serrano 61 ☎ 91 577 50 31 🚇 Rubén Dario

CENTRO COMERCIAL MADRID-2, LA VAGUADA
Madrid's largest and brashest mall centre, with over 350 stores. One floor has a cinema, discotheque and bars.

➕ D2 ✉ Monforte de Lemos 36 ☎ 91 730 10 00 🚇 Barrio del Pilar

CITYVIPS/VIPS
The 12 bright, bold VIPS stores around the city, convenient and impressive in size, sell books, magazines and records, food and gifts. Each also has a bar and restaurant.

➕ bl; D8 ✉ Gran Via 43 (with branches throughout the city) ☎ 91 559 64 57 🚇 Callao

EL CORTE INGLÉS
These four department stores dominate Spanish retail. They are so vast it is almost absurd, and you can buy almost anything. Services are available as well as goods and there's also a well-stocked supermarket. Information desks are staffed by multi-lingual assistants.

➕ F8 ✉ Calle Goya 76 (with branches at Calle Preciados 3; Calle Princesa 42; Raimundo Fernández Villaverde 79) ☎ 91 556 23 00 🚇 Goya

EL JARDÍN DE SERRANO
A small, elegant cluster of fashion and accessory stores in the heart of Madrid's fashionable *barrio Salamanca*.

➕ F8 ✉ Calle Goya 6–8 ☎ 91 577 04 06 🚇 Serrano

FNAC
Five floors of books and CDs, plus a small concert area where you can occasionally hear big names. Also has Spanish and foreign newspapers, photograph developing services and ticket agency.

➕ bl; D8 ✉ Calle Preciados 28 ☎ 91 595 62 00 🚇 Callao

GALERÍA DEL PRADO
A small, well-organised mall in the basement of the Palace Hotel. The 39 stores are mainly devoted to fashion.

➕ dll; E9 ✉ Plaza de las Cortes 7 🚇 Atocha

NEWSPAPER KIOSK IN PUERTA DEL SOL
This is the only one of the city's hundreds of bright, cheerful kiosks that is open 24 hours a day. It sells not only foreign newspapers and a startling range of pornography, but also academic studies of Nietzsche and Kant.

➕ bll; D9 ✉ Puerta del Sol 🚇 Sol

Shopping around
For better or worse, the retail scene in Madrid is increasingly dominated by chain stores and *centros comerciales* (shopping malls). Try and get into the back streets, to visit smaller establishments, and join the queue: shop assistants can be sloth-like when it comes to serving customers they don't know, and 'service with a smile' is only now starting to catch on. Larger stores are open through lunch, while smaller ones continue, in time-honoured fashion, to close from about 1:30 to about 4:30.

TRENDSETTERS

New Madrid fashion

Though not yet Paris, Rome, London or even Barcelona, Madrid is slowly gaining a foothold in the world of men's and women's fashion. The international success of Adolfo Domínguez has been followed by that of Roberto Verino, and together with the avant-garde designs of Agatha Ruiz de la Prada and Jesús del Pozo, the Spanish designers are proving a serious threat to the more established Italians. The *beau monde* does much of its shopping in the *barrio Salamanca*.

ADOLFO DOMÍNGUEZ

The work of Spain's best-known fashion designer is characterised by its beautiful, classic cut and its subdued colours. A men's shop is close by, at Calle Ortega y Gasset 4.

🞡 F6 ✉ Calle de Serrano 36 ☎ 91 576 70 53 🚇 Rubén Darío

AGATHA RUIZ DE LA PRADA

Agatha's daring, brightly coloured patchwork designs still fly the flag for the *movida*, that era in the mid-1980s when Madrid believed everything was there just to be enjoyed. Every Thursday at 8PM drinks are served; stop by to see what is happening.

🞡 E7 ✉ Calle Marques de Riscal 8 ☎ 91 310 44 83 🚇 Rubén Darío

ÁLVAREZ-GÓMEZ

A Madrid institution with more than 100 years in the perfume business. Manufactures its own in-house cologne.

🞡 E8 ✉ Calle de Serrano 14 ☎ 91 431 16 56 🚇 Serrano

ARMANI

The sobriety and elegance of this shop provides the best possible showcase for the clothes. An Emporio Armani is at Claudio Coello 77.

🞡 F7 ✉ Ortega y Gasset 16 ☎ 91 576 10 36 🚇 Nuñez de Balboa

EKSEPTION

Ekseption carries designs as in-your-face as the store's misspelled name – clothing from the likes of Jean Paul Gaultier, Dolce & Gabanna and Vivienne Westwood.

🞡 F8 ✉ Calle Velázquez 28 ☎ 91 577 4353 🚇 Velázquez

ESCADA

Marghareta Ley's German designs use bright colours in distinctive, unconventional ways.

🞡 F7 ✉ Calle Ortega y Gasset 21 ☎ 91 577 41 88 🚇 Nuñez de Balboa

FARRUTX

Has an international reputation for its shoes, made from the finest quality leather with designs to suit all tastes.

🞡 E8 ✉ Calle de Serrano 7 ☎ 91 576 94 93 🚇 Serrano

LOEWE

The Spanish design firm with the greatest international prestige is best known for its leather bags and fashion accessories.

🞡 E8 ✉ Calle de Serrano 26 ☎ 91 577 60 56 🚇 Serrano

ROBERTO VERINO

The simple, elegant lines of Verino's designs are a joy.

🞡 F8 ✉ Calle Claudio Coello 27 ☎ 91 577 73 81 🚇 Serrano

VACAS FLASCAS

Skinny Cows is an eye-catching fashion store run by two young women who are fast gaining an international reputation.

🞡 F7 ✉ Calle Claudio 24 ☎ 91 57 64 83 🚇 Serrano

ANTIQUES

BARRIO SALAMANCA

This area of the city contains over 50 antique shops – nine in Calle Claudio Coello, six in Nuñez de Balboa and four in Calle Velázquez. Particularly noteworthy are Sant-Yago (Calle Hermosilla 37), specialising in glassware; the Mercadillo Balboa (Nuñez de Balboa 63), a collection of auction houses under one roof which sell as well as auction; the Almodena Escudero (Príncipe de Vergara 28), and La Trastienda de Alcalá (Calle Alcalá 64), specialising in quality reproductions.
✚ F8 ✉ *Barrio Salamanca* 🚇 Serrano, Velázquez, Nuñez de Balboa, Príncipe de Vergara

CALLE DEL PRADO

Fifteen antique shops are concentrated in and around this street off Plaza de Santa Ana.
✚ dI–dII; D9–E9 ✉ Calle del Prado 🚇 Antón Martín

CENTRO DE ANTICUARIOS LAGASCA

The most interesting shops here are Lepina, Pedro Alarcón and Luis Carabe selling a broad range of stock.
✚ F8 ✉ Calle Lagasca 36 🚇 Serrano

GALERIAS PIQUER

This pleasant mall in the Rastro street market has 20 antique shops. Particularly worth a look are Siglo 20 for art deco; and El Estudio which sells Isabelline furniture and lamps.
✚ bIII; D9 ✉ Calle Ribera de Curtidores 29 🚇 La Latina

GALERÍAS RIVERA

The smallest of the antique malls in the Rastro street market, with just four shops.
✚ bIII; D9 ✉ Ribera de Curtidores 15 🚇 La Latina

HILDALGO

Devoted to the loving restoration of everyday objects of the past such as coffee machines and old-fashioned steam irons, this is a fascinating little store – on the main street of the Rastro flea market – that has been going for 50 years.
✚ bIII; D10 ✉ Ribera de Curtidores 29 🚇 La Latina

MERCADO PUERTA DE TOLEDO

Opened several years ago as a luxury shopping area, the Puerta de Toledo market has been an economic disaster, and its antique shops are always likely to close down. However, it is still worth a browse.
✚ aIV; D10 ✉ Puerta de Toledo ☎ 91 366 72 00 🚇 Puerta de Toledo

NUEVAS GALERÍAS

The third antiques mall in the Rastro street market, with 11 stores. Look for María Eugenia Falla (brass), González (bronze) and Sucesor de Cuenca (old office equipment). The restoration is always exemplary.
✚ bIII; D9 ✉ Ribera de Curtidores 12 🚇 La Latina

Where to go

Madrid's bewildering array of antique shops are in three main areas: the *barrio Salamanca*, around the Calle del Prado and Santa Ana, and around the Rastro, particularly down the Calle Ribera de Curtidores – the most likely source for bargains. Many shops do not specialise but sell a broad selection of merchandise.

OFFBEAT & UNUSUAL

Lucky dip

The little specialist shops of Madrid can offer much insight into the minds of the city's inhabitants. Sometimes the shop's layout is so irrational that it is hard to know what the place is really selling. You would not actually want to buy anything at some of these places — it's junk. Particularly in the area around the Plaza Mayor, the district of La Latina and the area between Calle del Barco and Calle Hortaleza, just off the Gran Via, it is worth pausing to admire offbeat window displays. These have been lovingly put together by proprietors who know they are as much a part of the urban landscape as any monument.

ALMORAIMA

A wide range of fans, from the cheap and cheerful to works of art. The most expensive is made of bone and marble and costs more than 50,000ptas.

➕ bll; D9 ✉ Plaza Mayor 12 ☎ 91 365 42 89 Ⓜ Sol

CARAMELES PACO

Devoted exclusively to boiled sweets, Carameles Paco sells sugary replicas of elephants, rabbits and a village square; the window display is unique.

➕ blll; D9 ✉ Calle Toledo 55 ☎ 91 365 42 58 Ⓜ La Latina

CASA JIMÉNEZ

The *mantillas* and shawls around the shoulders of Spanish women are one of the distinguishing dress features among women of a certain age. Casa Jiménez, has been selling them since 1923.

➕ bll; D9 ✉ Preciados 42 ☎ 91 548 05 26 Ⓜ Callao, Santo Domingo

CASA YUSTAS

This hat shop founded in 1894 retains its period charm, and the defiant lack of adornment and the lengthy counter, behind which four assistants stand rigidly to attention, typifies late 19th-century *madrileño* establishments.

➕ bll; D9 ✉ Plaza Mayor 30 ☎ 91 366 58 34 Ⓜ Sol

CORSETERÍA LA LATINA

Of the many lingerie shops around Madrid, this is the best with the most sizzling window display, an awe-inspiring collection of amazing outsized girdles.

➕ blll; D9 ✉ Calle Toledo 49 ☎ 91 365 46 22 Ⓜ La Latina

CURIOSITY SHOP

Inspired by the wacky world of 50s sci-fi. Eye-tricking lenses and lamps that create strange effects are among the oddities piled high inside.

➕ blll; D9 ✉ Calle Latoneros 1 ☎ 91 365 84 22 Ⓜ La Latina

DON JUAN

Benito Gómez opened Don Juan in 1995 and sells typical but authentic objects from all over Spain, to a slightly select market: look here for century-old *azulejo* tiles and *Rocío* perfume bottles.

➕ al; C8 ✉ Plaza de la Marina Española 7 ☎ 91 547 12 27 Ⓜ Opera

EL ELEFANTE BLANCO

A terrific store to visit with the kids; The White Elephant was opened in the late 1980s by a stilt-walker; and specialises in circus equipment. The shop assistants will demonstrate how the magic tricks work.

➕ cl–dl, D8–E8 ✉ Calle Infantas 5 ☎ 91 531 3350 Ⓜ Gran Via

FEKI

Feki has been making boxes of all sizes, shapes and colours since the 1970s. You can have them made to order.

✚ F8 ✉ Calle Hermosilla 56
☎ 91 431 73 35 Ⓜ Velázquez

JUSTO ALGABA
Bullfighters come here for their suits of lights and other bullfighting paraphernalia.
✚ cll; D9 ✉ Calle Paz 4
☎ 91 523 35 95 Ⓜ Sol

LEFTY'S COMPANY
As the name suggests, offers an easier world to left-handed people. There is a wide range of office and kitchen equipment on display, with highlights including reverse-design scissors and a wristwatch that runs backwards.
✚ F7 ✉ Calle de Serrano 162
☎ 91 41117 60 Ⓜ República Argentina

LUIS VILLASANTE
Luis Villasante specialises in material for religious habits and gives saints' names to its various shades of cloth – dark brown is 'Saint Francis of Assisi'. Other religious artefacts are also available and the window display, full of models of Baby Jesus, is fascinating. You'll find similar fare at Sobrina Pérez, a little further along Calle Postas.
✚ bll; D9 ✉ Calle Postas 14
☎ 91 366 46 40 Ⓜ Sol

PALACIOS Y MUSEOS
This unusual store sells items available elsewhere only from museums both Spanish and international. Everything is made by the same company that supplies the museums themselves.

✚ F8 ✉ Calle Velázquez 47
☎ 91 577 42 01 Ⓜ Velázquez

REGALOS AR
Regalos Ar is handily central and plentifully stocked with *lladró* (Spanish for porcelain) – that perennially popular souvenir. Also sells handicrafts and pearls from Majorca.
✚ cl; D8 ✉ Gran Vía 46
☎ 91 522 68 69 Ⓜ Callao

SESEÑA
This family establishment dating back to 1901, which keeps a firm eye on maintaining quality control, specialises in capes: Pablo Picasso, Michael Jackson and Hillary Clinton have all been customers.
✚ cll; D9 ✉ Calle de la Cruz 23 ☎ 91 531 68 40 Ⓜ Sol

LOS SIETE SOLES
Amulets and statuettes to ward off bad luck. The AIDUN statuette helps you to find a job, while TRI is said to protect married love.
✚ bll; D9 ✉ Calle Mayor 73
☎ 91 541 93 63
Ⓜ Sol/Opera

DE VIAJE
Opened in 1999, this story is unique in Madrid for offering everything the dedicated traveller could ever need – books, maps, hiking equipment and even cute little hand-warmers. Also organises hiking excursions.
✚ F8 ✉ Calle de Serrano 41
☎ 91 577 98 99 Ⓜ Serrano

Typically Spanish buying
Madrid is the best place in Spain to buy all kinds of typically Spanish products. Consider taking home a cape, a *boina* (a typical Spanish gentleman's cap), a *bota de vino* (leather wine container, from which the wine is poured at arm's length into the mouth), a typical *azulejo* tile or a bottle of olive oil.

BOOKS & RECORDS

Reading about Madrid

To get an insider's view of life in the Spanish capital, you could do worse than to read Madrid novels such as Benito Pérez Galdos' *Fortunata y Jacinta*, a work of Dickensian scope and depth set in 1860s Madrid; Arturo Barea's *The Forge*, a boyhood look at life before and during the Spanish Civil War; and Camilo José Cela's *The Hive*, post-Civil War Madrid through the eyes of the 1989 winner of the Nobel Prize for Literature. Cervantes's *Don Quixote*, the great oeuvre of Spain's Golden Age, mentions Madrid briefly. British journalist John Hooper's *The New Spaniards* is a perceptive overview of contemporary Spain. All are available in English.

BOOKSELLER'S

The capital's best English-language bookshop also sells imported magazines and Spanish and Latin-American literature in translation. Excellent children's section.

✚ E6 ✉ José Abascal 48 ☎ 91 442 79 59 Ⓜ Rubén Darío

CASA DEL LIBRO

The House of the Book claims to stock everything. It does not, but three rambling floors do manage to give an impression of comprehensiveness. The foreign literature section in this branch is well-stocked.

✚ bl; D8 ✉ Gran Via 29 ☎ 91 521 21 13 Ⓜ Gran Via

CUESTA DE MOYANO

Every Sunday at 10:30 the book stalls open up along the road to the Retiro from Atocha. Many books are modern and no cheaper than in the shops, but there is a smattering of second-hand books in other languages, and the occasional gem waiting to be found.

✚ E10 ✉ Calle Claudio Moyano (next to Botanical Gardens) Ⓜ Atocha

EL FLAMENCO VIVE

There is no doubt that flamenco lives inside Alberto Martínez's store, Spain's first devoted to flamenco. In addition to a good selection of music, there are books on flamenco history and much flamenco paraphernalia.

✚ all; D9 ✉ Calle Conde de Lemos 7 ☎ 91 547 39 17 Ⓜ Opera

THE INTERNATIONAL BOOKSHOP

Madrid's only non-Spanish-language second-hand bookstore is American-owned and centrally located, and stocks far more than old paperbacks. Though most books are in English, it deals in other languages too. Like all good bookshops, it has a resident cat, Petra.

✚ bl; D9 ✉ Calle Campomanes 13 ☎ 91 541 72 91 Ⓜ Santo Domingo, Opera

MADRID ROCK

Madrid's biggest and best record store. Three floors stock just about everything including imports, and there are video screens, listening booths and a ticket service. Smaller branches are in Calle Mayor and Calle San Martín.

✚ cl; D8 ✉ Gran Via 25 ☎ 91 523 26 52 Ⓜ Gran Via

PASAJES

Here there are two floors piled high with current French, German, Italian, Portuguese and English titles; prices are high. The travel section is small but well-chosen. Friendly, English-speaking staff and central location.

✚ E8 ✉ Calle Génova 3 ☎ 91 310 12 45 Ⓜ Alonso Martinez

FOOD & WINE

BURGOS EL PALACIO DE LOS QUESOS

The window display in The Cheese Palace is one of the capital's most mouth-watering. Established in 1919.

✚ bII; D9 ✉ Calle Mayor 53 ☎ 91 548 16 23 🚇 Sol

CAFÉS POZO

The original of Madrid's three Cafés Pozo stores sells a wide range of coffees blended to order.

✚ cIII; D9 ✉ Calle Magdalena 23 ☎ 91 369 07 64 🚇 Antón Martín

CASA LARREINA

A wine supermarket, Casa Larreina offers probably the broadest selection of wines in Madrid – *all* the Spanish wines as well as a healthy foreign selection, and at prices lower than in many other shops. Another branch at Calle Francisco de Rojas 1.

✚ F7 ✉ Calle Padilla 42 ☎ 91 577 62 73 🚇 Nuñez de Balboa

LA MALLORQUINA

The aromas of Madrid's most central pastry shop have been greeting people emerging from the Sol metro for years. The custard-filled *napolitanas*, still hot from the oven, are a treat.

✚ cII; D9 ✉ Puerta del Sol 8 ☎ 91 521 12 01 🚇 Sol

MARIANO MADRUEÑO

Founded in 1895, this is one of the city's more traditional wine-shops or *bodegas*, with the original attractive wrought-iron and carved wood fittings. Reasonable.

✚ bII; D8 ✉ Postigo de San Martín 3 ☎ 91 521 19 55 🚇 Callao

MÉNDEZ

Marvel at the extraordinary selection of regional produce from the north of Spain including Cabrales cheese, lamprey, Padrón peppers and its own bread, baked in the Galician style.

✚ F8 ✉ Ayala 65 ☎ 91 402 43 78 🚇 Lista

MUSEO DEL JAMÓN

There are five branches of the Ham Museum in the city, each a spectacular testament to the fact that vegetarianism in Spain has a long way to go. *Jamón serrano* is the most popular, while *jamón de Jabugo*, at around 8,000ptas a kilo, is the crown jewel.

✚ cI; E9 ✉ Carrera de San Jerónimo 6 ☎ 91 521 03 46/57 21 🚇 Sol

LA OLEOTECA

Olive oil is the base of much Spanish cooking and makes a good gift. This store carries more than 60 different wonderful oils from all over Spain, as well as olives and vinegars – and even an olive oil soap bar.

✚ F4 ✉ Calle Juan Ramón Jiménez 37 ☎ 91 577 46 62 🚇 Cuzco

RESERVA Y CATA

Opened in 1998, this *bodega* (wine store) offers 600 hundred wines of mainly Spanish origin.

✚ D6 ✉ Calle Ramiro II 13 ☎ 91 553 04 02 🚇 Cuzco

Wine, cheese and *chorizo*

Spanish wine is slowly acquiring an international reputation, but Spanish cheese is not, although much of it is very good. The most typical is Manchego, which varies tremendously in quality, while the strongest is Cabrales, made from a mixture of sheep's and goat's milk. In addition to the hams, the Spanish sausages known as *chorizos* and the *morcill* (black puddings) are worth sampling.

77

LATE-NIGHT BARS (*CERVECERÍAS*)

Madrid by night

With almost 4,000 places to have a drink, Madrid can claim to be Europe's finest city for sheer variety of places available late into the night – sometimes very late indeed. Main bar areas in the centre are the start of the Paseo de la Castellana (sophisticated), Malasaña (thoroughly unsophisticated), Santa Ana (somewhere in between) and Chueca (gay).

BAGELÜS
Glitzy BageLüs includes a café, restaurant, record and bookshop and several bars. Regular live shows and cabaret.
☒ E6 ✉ Calle Maria de Molina 25 ☎ 91 561 61 00 ⏰ Open 24 hours Ⓜ Avenida de América

CERVECERÍA ALEMANA
One of the city's most popular bars is always bustling with smart, efficient waiters. A good meeting-place in the Santa Ana district.
☒ cll; D9 ✉ Plaza de Santa Ana 6 ☎ 91 429 70 33 Ⓜ Antón Martín

LA COQUETTE
The only Madrid bar dedicated exclusively to blues is very 1960s and very studenty.
☒ D9 ✉ Calle de las Hileras 14 Ⓜ Opera

LA CRIPTA MÀGICA
A little off the beaten track and a little offbeat – the drinks come with a magic show thrown in. For a long time, entry was by password only, but now it is open to all.
☒ dIV; E10 ✉ Calle de Tarragona 15 Ⓜ Palos de la Frontera

LA ESCONDIDA
Probably the smallest bar you have ever seen, with a wide range of wines and tasty *tapas*.
☒ bIII; D9 ✉ Plaza de Puerta Cerrada 6 ☎ 91 308 54 13 Ⓜ La Latina

FINNEGAN'S
Of the several popular Irish bars and clubs currently doing great business in Madrid, this unpretentious favourite comes the closest to authenticity. Fixtures and fittings are imported – the bar used to be the counter of a draper's in County Cork.
☒ E8 ✉ Plaza de las Salesas 9 ☎ 91 310 05 21 Ⓜ Chueca

LIBERTAD 8
A very relaxed watering-hole with nightly cabaret, plenty of seating and lots of cigarette smoke.
☒ dI; E8 ✉ Calle Libertad 8 ☎ 91 532 11 50 ⏰ Daily 11:30PM Ⓜ Chueca

REPORTER
Despite regular threats of closure, Reporter's convivial rear *terraza* still manages to open each year when summer arrives. Serves food at lunchtime.
☒ dIII; E9 ✉ Calle Fúcar 6 ☎ 91 429 39 22 Ⓜ Antón Martín

TORITO
This remarkable bar is tiny and cramped, with walls covered in bizarre montages. Non-Spaniards love the place since most of the music is Spanish.
☒ E8 ✉ Calle Pelayo 4 ☎ 91 532 77 99 Ⓜ Chueca

VIVA MADRID
The tiled *azulejo* frontage of the Santa Ana district's Viva Madrid has been photographed for a thousand guide books.
☒ cll; D9 ✉ Calle Manuel Fernández y González 7 ☎ 91 429 36 40 Ⓜ Antón Martín

Terrazas & Cocktail Bars

EL CHICOTE

Opened in 1931, El Chicote is the granddaddy of Madrid's *coctelerías*, and continues to be a nocturnal reference point for the rich and famous. Legend has it that the Chicote's *mojito* was Ernest Hemingway's favourite tipple. Art-deco fixtures and alcove seating make the Chicote a memorable, if rather expensive, experience.

✚ bl; D8 ✉ Gran Via 12 ☎ 91 532 67 37 🚇 Gran Via

DEL DIEGO

Del Diego's superb design and highly attentive bar staff have quickly made it one of Madrid's big three *coctelerías* or cocktail bars, along with El Chicote and Le Cock, two minutes away.

✚ cl; E8 ✉ Calle de la Reina 12 ☎ 91 523 31 06 🚇 Gran Via

DESTRÁS DEL PRADO

As its name (behind the Prado) suggests, a cocktail bar nestling in a back street between the Prado and the Retiro Park. Pleasant, warm-toned interior and low-key ambience. Reasonably priced.

✚ E9 ✉ Calle de Alberto Bosch 14 🚇 Retiro

LAS VISTILLAS

The *terraza* with the best night views. To find a quiet corner descend the steps to the area below the Viaduct.

✚ alll; C9 ✉ Travesía de las Vistillas 🚇 La Latina

PASEO DE LA CASTELLANA

Collectively known as the Costa Castellana, the stretch has about 20 *terrazas* between Atocha and the Plaza de Lima. They run right up the middle of the street; with the traffic whizzing by on either side and music booming out, they are not places for the hard-of-hearing or quietly spoken. Of the 20-odd *terrazas* here, not all are open from one year to the next. Perhaps the best are Bavaro Beach (Paseo del Prado), Bolero (Paseo de la Castellana 33) and Boulevard (Paseo de la Castellana 37).

✚ E9; E8; E7 ✉ Paseo del Prado; Paseo de Recoletos; Paseo de la Castellana 🚇 Atocha, Banco de España

PASEO DE PINTOR ROSALES

The *terrazas* here run along the side of the Parque del Oeste. Noisy and lots of fun.

✚ C8; C7 ✉ Paseo de Pintor Rosales 🚇 April–October 🚇 Plaza de España, Ventura Rodríguez

PLAZA DE CONDE DE BARAJAS

Just behind the Plaza Mayor, away from the traffic, without music and with a whole square to itself, this is the most peaceful of the *terrazas*. Open only in summer.

✚ bll; D9 ✉ Plaza de Conde de Barajas 🚇 Sol, Opera

Terrazas

Young *madrileños* go to *terraza* bars (that is, just about any bar with chairs and tables outside) to show off their suntans and drink late into the night. It is entirely logical that between April and late October, with temperatures in the upper 30s centigrade, bar culture should move outside and the streets and squares are hectic, heaving and fun.

OPERA & CLASSICAL MUSIC

Zarzuela

In the words of Edmundo de Amici, writing in 1870, the *zarzuela* is 'a piece of music somewhere between comedy and melodrama, between opera and vaudeville, with prose and verse, both recited and sung, serious and light-hearted, a very Spanish and very entertaining musical form'. Among theatre audiences of a certain age, it remains as popular as ever.

AUDITORIO NACIONAL DE MÚSICA

Madrid's finest classical music venue and the only one which can claim to be on the international classical music circuit is home to the Spanish National Orchestra, the ONE. It runs several seasons each year, the most important of which is the ONE's own October–June season. Good acoustics in circle seats.

🚇 F5 ✉ Príncipe de Vergara 146 ☎ 91 337 01 00 Ⓜ Cruz del Rayo

CENTRO CULTURAL DE LA VILLA

A multi-arts complex which occasionally offers classical recitals by visiting international musicians in contemporary design surroundings.

🚇 E8 ✉ Plaza de Colón ☎ 91 575 60 80 Ⓜ Colón

CIRCULO DE BELLAS ARTES

This is the best forum for contemporary classical music, with its own ensemble, the Grupo Círculo.

🚇 dII; E9 ✉ Calle Marqués de Casa Riera 2 ☎ 91 531 77 00/532 44 38 Ⓜ Banco de España

LA CORRALA

Though not a concert venue in the ordinary sense, during the summer La Corrala is used as an outdoor location for *zarzuela* performances.

🚇 cIV; D10 ✉ Calle Tribulete 12 ☎ No phone: see press for details Ⓜ Lavapiés

LA FÍDULA

Music students give recitals on most week nights between September and June.

🚇 dIII; E9 ✉ Calle Huertas 57 ☎ 91 429 29 47 Ⓜ Antón Martín

TEATRO MONUMENTAL

The place where classical concerts are recorded for broadcast by the Spanish Radio and Televison Orchestra and Choir.

🚇 dIII; E9 ✉ Calle Atocha 65 ☎ 91 429 81 19/12 81 Ⓜ Antón Martín

TEATRO PRADILLO

The best venue in Madrid for world music, and anything else off the musical beaten track. It also hosts improvisation evenings and performance art.

🚇 G5 ✉ Calle Pradillo 12 ☎ 91 416 90 11 Ⓖ See press for details Ⓜ Concha Espina

TEATRO REAL

The grandest and most beautiful of the European opera houses.

🚇 aII; C9 ✉ Plaza de Isabel II Ⓜ Opera

TEATRO DE LA ZARZUELA

Zarzuela is the *raison d'être* for this beautiful 1,300-seat hall. While the Teatro Real was under renovation, it was also Madrid's official opera house but now also hosts ballet and lesser known operatic work not found at the Real.

🚇 dII; E9 ✉ Calle Jovellanos 4 ☎ 91 429 82 25/524 54 00 Ⓜ Banco de España

FLAMENCO, ROCK & JAZZ

AQUALUNG
Madrid's main rock venue, in the La Ermita leisure complex, Aqualung is as likely to host performances by visiting British and American rock bands as Spanish.

🞣 B9 ✉ Paseo del la Ermita del Santon 40–8 ☎ 91 470 23 62 🚇 Pirámides, Marqués de Vadillo

BAR CAFÉ DEL FORO
Though it does mount straight rock, the Café del Foro also has salsa, fusion and cabaret as well as occasional magic and comedy shows. Friendly and buzzing venue.

🞣 D7 ✉ Calle San Andrés 38 ☎ 91 445 37 52 🚇 Bilbao

CAFÉ CENTRAL
One of the best jazz venues in Europe. There are performances every night mainly from Spanish, but sometimes foreign, musicians.

🞣 cIII; D9 ✉ Plaza del Ángel 10 ☎ 91 369 41 43 🕐 Daily 10:30PM 🚇 Sevilla, Antón Martín, Sol

CAFÉ POPULART
Live music every day – jazz, blues and swing – in a comfortable environment where the conversation is always intelligent.

🞣 cII; E9 ✉ Calle Huertas 22 ☎ 91 429 84 07 🚇 Antón Martín

CANDELA
Candela's clientele are mainly gypsies from the surrounding *barrio*, the music is exclusively flamenco, and the atmosphere is highly charged, particularly after two in the morning.

🞣 cIII; D9 ✉ Calle del Olmo at corner of Calle Olivar 🚇 Antón Martín

CASA PATAS
The best-known of Madrid's flamenco *tablaos* is a little touristy but nonetheless it is enjoyable. Live midnight performances, more frequently held in May.

🞣 cIII; D9 ✉ Calle Cañizares 10 ☎ 91 369 15 74/04 96 🕐 Thu–Sat midnight 🚇 Tirso de Molina, Antón Martín

CLAMORES JAZZ
Jazz is still at the heart of this elegant nightclub but it now features tango and even karaoke. Live music each night.

🞣 D7 ✉ Calle Alburquerque 14 ☎ 91 445 79 38 🕐 Daily 10PM 🚇 Bilbao

EL DESPERTAR
A jazz bar during the week with live concerts at weekends. The wildly bearded owner of this intimate late-night joint seems to know absolutely everything about jazz.

🞣 cIII; D9 ✉ Calle Torrecilla del Leal ☎ 91 530 77 80 95 🕐 Fri–Sat evenings 🚇 Antón Martín

REVÓLVER CLUB
This large rock club, one of the favoured venues of visiting indie bands, hosts flamenco performances on Monday nights.

🞣 D7 ✉ Calle Galileo 26 ☎ 91 594 27 05/26 38/26 79 🚇 Quevedo, Argüelles

More rock than flamenco
Madrid's rock venues continue to offer lucky visitors the chance to see performers who usually play much larger places in relatively intimate surroundings. Prices of tickets are not unreasonable although you might not say the same of drinks. Surprisingly, there are few flamenco bars.

CLUBS & DISCOS

Rave on

The limitless capacity of *madrileños* for having fun has made Madrid a disco-owner's dream. The city is the undisputed European nightlife capital, and the night begins and ends very late indeed.

ARCHY

This extremely fashionable club and restaurant has a well-known clientele, with a disco in the basement and an intimate bar-restaurant upstairs. And it's as good for talking as for dancing.

🔜 E7 ⊠ Calle Marqués de Riscal 11 ☎ 91 308 31 62/27 36/21 62 🚇 Quevedo; Iglésia

EL SOL

Chaotic and a bit shabby, but lots of fun, El Sol was big in *movida* Madrid. You'll find a wide choice of music. Central location.

🔜 cl; D9 ⊠ Calle Jardines 3 ☎ 91 532 64 90 🚇 Sol, Gran Via

EMPIRE

The space is original with five bars on two floors: from above you look down on the people dancing. The clientele is in the 25 to 35 age group.

🔜 dl; E8 ⊠ Paseo de Recoletos 16 ☎ 91 447 01 28 🚇 Colón

JOY ESCLAVA

Plush, though not forbiddingly stylish. The central location attracts a diverse clientele.

🔜 bll; D9 ⊠ Calle Arenal 11 ☎ 91 366 54 39/32 84/37 33 🚇 Ópera

PALACE DISCOTHEQUE

Telephones on each table let you call another table and offer a drink or a dance to someone who has caught your eye. The house band is a rarity.

🔜 bll; D9 ⊠ Plaza de Isabel II, 7 ☎ 91 541 82 30 🚇 Ópera

PALACIO DE GAVIRIA

One of Madrid's more remarkable night-time locations. An 1851 palace, with fixtures and fittings generally intact, it reopened in 1981 as a nightspot. With its grand staircase entrance and 14 halls spread over 1,300sq m it is well worth checking out.

🔜 bll; D9 ⊠ Calle Arenal 9 ☎ 91 526 60 69 🚇 Sol

PACHÁ

This is a standby of the macro-disco scene. A wild and wonderful blend of visual styles among its clientele, all to hard, driving dance music. Its central location makes it popular with foreign visitors.

🔜 D8 ⊠ Callede Barceló 11 ☎ 91 526 60 69 🚇 Sol

SCALA MELÍA CASTILLA

The closest Madrid comes to Paris' Crazy Horse, with old-fashioned cabaret shows with a meal twice daily.

🔜 E4 ⊠ Capitán Haya 43 (Edificio Meliá Castilla) ☎ 91 571 44 11 🕓 Closed Aug 🚇 Cuzco, Valdeacederas

TEATRIZ

A bar, restaurant and nightclub in one, this complex of avant-garde rooms designed by Philippe Starck in the late 1980s is incredible to look at, if a little cold when not packed.

🔜 F8 ⊠ Calle Hermosilla 15 ☎ 91 577 53 79/91 95 🚇 Serrano

CINEMAS

ALPHAVILLE
Alphaville, opened shortly after democracy came to Spain, still shows short films before the main feature, showcasing talent that might otherwise go unrecognised. Late-night showings at weekends and a good café downstairs.
✚ C8 ✉ Calle Martín de los Heros 14 ☎ 91 559 38 36 Ⓜ Plaza de España

FILMOTECA ESPAÑOLA
Inaugurated in 1922 as the Cine Doré and lovingly re-created in 1989, the Filmoteca shows four original version films daily in two theatres. Many films are classics: others are truly obscure, but most have something to recommend them, and it is worth taking a chance. Tickets may be three times cheaper than anywhere else. A good bookshop as well as pleasant bar are in the foyer.
✚ cIII; E9 ✉ Calle Santa Isabel 3 ☎ 91 369 11 25 Ⓜ Antón Martín

IDEAL MULTICINES
Madrid's most comfortable cinema has eight theatres of varied size showing art and mainstream features. Weekend late-night showings.
✚ cIII; D9 ✉ Calle Doctor Cortezo 6 ☎ 91 369 25 18/03 31 Ⓜ Sol, Tirso de Molina

OPEN-AIR CINEMA
In summer two locations – one in the Parque de Oeste, the other in the Casa de Campo – offer open-air cinema at good prices. Normally only in Spanish.
✚ B7–B8 ✉ Parque de la Mombilla, Avienda de Villadoid ☎ 91 541 37 21 Ⓜ Príncipe Pío
✚ B8–B9 ✉ La Pipa – Avienda de Portugal ☎ 91 798 17 60 Ⓜ Lago

PRINCESA
Since it opened in the mid 1990s, this has become the city's main screening point for new Spanish films and a good place to sample the burgeoning local film industry.
✚ D7–D8 ✉ Calle Princesa 3 ☎ 91541 41 00 Ⓜ Plaza de España

RENOIR
The best of cinemas clustered around the bottom of Calle Martín de los Heros near the Plaza de España, shows the latest art films in five theatres of differing sizes. Detailed information sheets are published (in Spanish) to accompany each film. In the Plaza de España theatre there is a good cinema bookshop, open during the week and there are late-night showings at weekends.
✚ C8 ✉ Calle Martín de los Heros 12 ☎ 91 559 57 60 Ⓜ Plaza de España
A newer Renoir is in Cuatro Caminos ✉ Calle Raimundo Fernández Villaverde 10 ☎ 91 534 00 77 Ⓜ Cuatro Caminos

On the increase
While the Spanish film industry is burgeoning, the number of cinemas is also on the increase, with 60 at the last count. Most cinemas have a *día del espectador*, or audience day, which might be a Monday or a Wednesday, when tickets are half the normal price. Always arrive well in advance for mid- and late-evening weekend showings, particularly if a film has just opened; queues start forming as much as an hour before projection time. Bigger cinemas now have advanced booking and most have reserved seating at weekends. Cinema information is published in full in all the daily newspapers: earliest showings (*pasos*) are generally at 4, latest at 10.30.

Original version
Ten of Madrid's cinemas show exclusively original version films without dubbing:
Bellas Artes ✉ Calle Marqués de Casa Riera 2 ☎ 522 50 92
Rosales ✉ Calle Quintana 22 ☎ 541 58 00
Ideal Yelmo Cineplex ✉ Calle Doctor Cortezo 6 ☎ 91 369 2518
Luna ✉ Calle Luna 2 ☎ 91 522 4752

LUXURY HOTELS

Prices

For a double room expect to pay

Luxury	over 25,000ptas
Mid-range	7,000–20,000ptas
Budget	under 7,000ptas

Add 7 per cent VAT to all prices. Many hotels in all price categories offer bargain weekend rates.

Paradores

Spain's network of *paradores*, sumptuous aristocratic residences converted into luxury hotels, is no longer a well-kept secret but there are none in Madrid. Information and reservations about those elsewhere ✉ Calle Requéna 3 ☎ 91 516 67 00

EUROBUILDING

With 600 rooms and twin towers, this is the largest hotel in Madrid and an example of what the Madrid of the future will look like. Located at the non-touristy, business end of the city, Euro-building is a world unto itself, part of a complex with shops, clubs, cafés, a gym and sauna.
🛏 F4 ✉ Calle Padre Damián 23 ☎ 91 345 45 00, fax 91 531 31 27 Ⓜ Cuzco

GRAN HOTEL REINA VICTORIA

Facing the Teatro Español in the heart of the buzzing Santa Ana district, the magnificent 201-room Reina Victoria has historical connections with the bullfighting world.
🛏 dII; D9 ✉ Plaza de Santa Ana 14 ☎ 91 531 45 00, fax 91 429 4036 Ⓜ Sol

MELÍA MADRID

The centrally located 275-room Melía, a 20-storey building, is modern, functional and extremely spacious, with gym and sauna.
🛏 C7 ✉ Calle Princesa 27 ☎ 91 541 82 00, fax 91 541 1988 Ⓜ Ventura Rodríguez

PALACE

Long in competition with the Ritz as Madrid's best central hotel, the 440-room, Palace, opened in 1913, is a little less formal and is popular with visiting celebrities.
🛏 dII; E9 ✉ Plaza de las Cortes 7 ☎ 91 360 80 00, fax 91 360 81 00 Ⓜ Banco de España

RITZ

Spain's first luxury hotel, opened in 1910, lives up to its name and reputation with 152 luxurious rooms. Between spring and autumn there's a delightful terrace-restaurant.
🛏 dII; E9 ✉ Plaza de la Lealtad 5 ☎ 91 521 28 57, fax 91 523 87 76 Ⓜ Banco de España

SANTO MAURO

This small hotel in the French-style former palace of the Dukes of Santo Mauro has a lovely patio entrance and a swimming pool. The 37 avant-garde rooms are all different, fresh and inviting.
🛏 E7 ✉ Calle Zurbano 36 ☎ 91 319 69 00, fax 91 308 54 77 Ⓜ Rubén Darío

VILLA MAGNA

With French neo-classical decor and the excellent restaurant (Berceo), the Villa Magna is favoured by visiting businessmen for its location at the start of the Castellana.
🛏 E7 ✉ Paseo de la Castellana 22 ☎ 91 576 75 00, fax 91 575 95 04 Ⓜ Rubén Darío

WELLINGTON

The 274-room Wellington, in the elegant *barrio Salamanca*, is the closest luxury hotel to the Retiro Park. A flamenco venue, Zambra, is downstairs.
🛏 F8 ✉ Calle Velázquez 8 ☎ 91 575 44 00, fax 91 576 41 64 Ⓜ Retiro

MID-RANGE HOTELS

AROSA
Very central, the Arosa has long been popular with visitors, particularly families, and makes an excellent base.

➕ d; D8 ✉ Calle de la Salud 21 ☎ 91 532 16 00, fax 91 531 31 27 Ⓜ Sol

ASTURIAS
Convenient to the Puerta del Sol, the 175-room Asturias is close to the main sights and nightlife. Ask for an inside room if you're particularly sensitive to noise.

➕ d; D9 ✉ Calle Sevilla 2 ☎ 91 429 66 76, fax 91 429 40 36 Ⓜ Sevilla

CARLOS V
The 67-room Carlos V is clean and bright and is next to the Puerta del Sol. If you can get a room on the fifth floor you will get a balcony.

➕ b/l; D9 ✉ Calle Maestro Vitoria 5 ☎ 91 531 41 00, fax 91 531 37 61 Ⓜ Sol

CONDE DUQUE
Giving onto an enclosed square, the 143-room Conde Duque is among the more peaceful hotels near the city centre.

➕ D7 ✉ Plaza del Conde Valle Suchil 5 ☎ 91 447 70 00, fax 91 448 35 69 Ⓜ San Bernardo

EL PRADO
Within easy reach of the Prado and the Santa Ana district, this lovely building was restored in 1992. Windows are double-glazed, ensuring a good night's sleep.

➕ c/l; E9 ✉ Calle Prado 11 ☎ 91 369 02 34, fax 91 429 28 29 Ⓜ Antón Martín, Sevilla

GALIANO RESIDENCIA
Once a noble family's palace, the 29-room Galiano is small, but its spacious rooms and old-world feel make it one of Madrid's better-kept secrets. Quiet location.

➕ E8 ✉ Calle Alcalá Galiano 6 ☎ 91 319 20 00/522 10 13, fax 91 319 99 14 Ⓜ Colón

INGLÉS
The clean 58-room family-owned Inglés is pleasantly located in a maze of narrow streets within easy reach of many sights.

➕ d; D9 ✉ Calle Echegaray 8 ☎ 91 429 65 51, fax 91 420 24 23 Ⓜ Sevilla

MÓNACO
The Monaco retains much charm, particularly in its intimate lobby, and some of its 32 rooms are supremely kitsch.

➕ d/l; E8 ✉ Calle Barbieri 5 ☎ 91 522 46 30, fax 91 521 16 01 Ⓜ Chueca

PARIS
Centrally located with 120 rooms, half of which are air-conditioned, the hotel offers all the basic facilities. Delightful interior courtyard.

➕ F8 ✉ Calle Goya 79 ☎ 435 75 45, fax 91 531 01 88 Ⓜ Goya

PINTOR
The Hawaiian-style lobby of this hotel is probably Madrid's tackiest, but the 170 rooms are comfortable and the location is good for shopping.

➕ F8 ✉ Calle Goya 79 ☎ 914 35 75 45, fax 91 431 09 43 Ⓜ Goya

Booking
Madrid has many hotels, and finding a room should not be hard except in tourist areas. Book as far in advance as possible, and call to reconfirm. If you arrive without a reservation, contact the accommodation agency called Brújula (✉ Head Office: Calle Princesa 1, 6th floor ☎ 91 559 97 05/9–7), which will book rooms in Madrid hotels for 300ptas. The phone is often busy, so go in person either to the head office or to one of the branches. They're at Atocha (🕐 8AM–10PM) and the Chamartín Railway Station (🕐 7AM–11:30PM).

BUDGET ACCOMMODATION

Things to note

It is worth remembering that at the lower end of the scale a good *hostal* may be more comfortable than a poor hotel. All the places on this page of this guide are *hostales*. Prices can vary according to season.

ARMESTO

A particularly friendly *hostal* opposite the Plaza de la Cortes. The owners have made an attempt to keep the rooms well-decorated.

✚ dII; E9 ✉ Calle San Agustín 6 (1st floor derecha) ☎ 91 429 90 31 Ⓜ Antón Martín

CERVANTES

This family-owned *hostal* is in a quiet area near the Retiro and the Prado. All 18 rooms have private bath. Don't be put off by the rickety lift.

✚ dII; E9 ✉ Calle Cervantes 34 (2nd floor) ☎ 91 429 27 45/429 83 65, 91 429 27 45 Ⓜ Antón Martín

EUROPA

Offering slightly more than the average budget hotel, including hair-dryers and satellite TV. All rooms are en-suite. Central location.

✚ C8 ✉ Calle del Cármen 4 ☎ 91 521 29 00 Ⓜ Callao

LA MONTAÑA

There are five *hostales* at this address in a relatively peaceful area east of the centre. Rooms are decent-sized and well-lit.

✚ C8 ✉ Calle Juan Álvarez Mendizabal 44 (4th floor) ☎ 91 547 10 88 Ⓜ Ventura Rodríguez

LORENZO

The Lorenzo is most notable for its soundproof windows. It is quite stylish if not very homely.

✚ cI; E8 ✉ Calle Infantas 26 (3rd floor) ☎ 91 521 30 57 Ⓜ Gran Vía

RETIRO/NARVÁEZ

In these two *hostales* in the same building, all rooms have showers, but not all have a toilet. Though a little way from the centre, they are easily accessible by public transport. The Retiro has 16 rooms, the Narváez 11.

✚ F8 ✉ Calle O'Donnell 27 (4th floor derecha and 5th floor) ☎ 91 576 00 37/575 01 07 Ⓜ Príncipe de Vergara

RIESCO

This family run *hostal* has 27 hotel rooms at *hostal* prices. It is just off the Plaza del Sol – you can't get much more central than that.

✚ bII; D9 ✉ Calle Correo 2 (3rd floor) ☎ 91 522 26 92 Ⓜ Sol

SUD AMERICANA

Although this is very small (with only eight rooms), it's ideal if you plan to spend a lot of time around the Prado. All rooms have showers, (not all have a bath), and there are pleasant views. The Hostal Coruña, in the same building, is slightly less appealing.

✚ dIII; E9 ✉ Paseo del Prado 12 (6th floor) ☎ 91 429 25 64 Ⓜ Antón Martín, Atocha

PAZ

Some rooms of this *hostal* on a quiet street overlook a shady courtyard. It's very clean, very efficient and very friendly.

✚ bII; D9 ✉ Calle Flora 4 (1st floor) ☎ 91 547 30 47 Ⓜ Sol, Opera

MADRID
travel facts

ARRIVING & DEPARTING

Before you go

- Visitors from Belgium, France, Germany, Luxembourg, the Netherlands and Portugal do not need a passport, and have the same rights as in their own country. Visitors to Spain from Britain require a valid passport in the absence of a British ID card.
- Visas are not required for UK, US, Canadian, New Zealand, Eire or other EU nationals for stays of under 90 days. Australian nationals visiting Spain do require a visa. Ask the nearest Spanish Consulate for information.
- Vaccinations are not required unless you are coming from a known infected area.
- EU nationals are entitled to health care under EU law, if they have an E111 form, but it is safer (and quicker) to take out full health and travel insurance before leaving. Non-EU residents should take out private medical and travel insurance before leaving.

When to go

- April to early July and mid-September to mid-November are the best.
- July and August are very hot with temperatures of 31 centigrade.
- January and February are the quietest months but can be cold.

Climate

- Winter lasts from early December until the end of February.
- March can be damp and unpleasant.
- Summers are hot and dry: rain is unusual between June and October.
- Spring and autumn are lovely with little rain, blue skies and a pleasant temperatures.

Arriving by air

- All flights arrive at Barajas Airport. The Spanish airline is Iberia.
- Barajas information ☎ 393 60 00
  Iberia information (Infolberia)
  ☎ 902 4000 500
  Flight information
  ☎ 305 83 43/ 44/45
- A bus leaves Barajas 🕒 5AM–midnight every 15 minutes (look for EMT signs). It arrives at an area directly beneath the Plaza de Colón. To get from here to the Colón metro, you have to go up to street level and cross the square, a five-minute walk. There is a metro link to the airport (Aeropuerto, line 8) – it's a 30-minute ride from the centre, but you will have to change lines at least once. A taxi from the airport to the city centre takes around 20 minutes and costs 400ptas.

Arriving by train

- Trains from France, Portugal and Northern Spain arrive at Chamartín Station.
- Trains from southern and eastern Spain and express services from Lisbon arrive at Atocha Station. Both are on the metro system.
- Between Chamartín and Atocha are two other stations, Recoletos and Nuevos Ministerios, where you can get off trains but not board them.

Arriving by car

- Two ring roads circle Madrid: an outer one (M40) and an inner (M30). Head for Paseo de la Castellana: this is central Madrid's main artery, and most central locations are easily reached from here.

Arriving by bus

- There are many private bus companies in Spain. Many pass through the Estación Sur de Autobuses on Calle Méndez Alvaro, which is near the Méndez Alvaro metro station.

Customs regulations

- Provided it is for personal use only EU nationals can bring back as much as they like, although the following guidelines should be adhered to as customs may wish to know why you are taking home more: 800 cigarettes, 400 cigarillos, 200 cigars, 1kg of tobacco, 10 litres of spirits, 20 litres of fortified wine, 90 litres of wine and 110 litres of beer.
- The limits for US citizens and for all other non-EU visitors are 200 cigarettes or 100 small cigars or 250g of tobacco; 1 litre of alcohol (over 22 percent alcohol) or 2 litres of fortified wine; 50g of perfume.

ESSENTIAL FACTS

Electricity

- The standard current is 220 volts.
- Plugs are of round two-pin type.
- Travel plugs can be found at Corte Inglés department stores.

Etiquette

- Though they do not normally form orderly queues, Spaniards are generally aware of their place in the service order.
- Though there are clearly marked 'No Smoking' areas in many restaurants, many Spaniards smoke and their smoke fills the restaurant anyway. Smoking on public transport is banned.
- Stretching and yawning in public is considered vulgar.
- Do not be worried about using your voice to attract attention in bars and restaurants say 'Oiga' Oh-ee-ga (literally 'hear me'). You may be ignored if you don't.
- In restaurants, it can take longer to get the bill than the meal; be prepared if you're in a rush and make sure to ask for the bill when ordering your final course.
- Drinks are normally paid for before you leave the bar, not on a round by round basis.
- Tipping is discretionary, but leaving around 10 per cent is normal practice.

Money matters

- The Spanish currency is the peseta, abbreviated to pta.
- Notes: 1,000ptas, 2,000ptas, 5,000ptas, 10,000ptas.
- Coins: 1pta, 5 ptas (new style: small bronze known informally as duros); 10ptas (rare); 25ptas (small bronze, with hole); 50, 100 , 200 and 500ptas.
- On 1 January 1999 the euro became the official currency of Spain and the Spanish pesata became a denomination of the euro. The Spanish notes and coins continue to be legal tender during a transitional period. Euro bank notes and coins are likely to be introduced by 1 January 2002.
- Most major travellers' cheques can be changed at banks. American Express offers best travellers' cheque rates.
- Credit cards are now accepted in all large establishments and an increasing number of smaller ones.
- There are many multi-lingual cash points: ServiRed and TeleBanco take all major credit cards.

Opening hours

- Shops: 9–1:30, 5–8
- Department stores: 9–9
- Churches: 9:30–1:30, 5–7:30
- Museums: considerable variation, but many close on Mondays
- Banks: Mon–Fri 9–2; between October and May many banks open from 9–1 on Saturdays.
- Some small shops open on Sundays with big malls and stores allowed to open on eight Sundays

a year and on four of the public holidays. They usually choose the run up to Christmas to open but opening times are well advertised.

Places of worship
- Dress formally: do not wear shorts.
- Do not enter during Mass.
- Flash photography is not normally permitted.

Public holidays
- 1 Jan: New Year's Day
  6 Jan: Epiphany
  Good Friday
  Easter Monday
  1 May: Labour Day
  2 May: Madrid Day
  15 May: San Isidro
  15 Aug: Virgen de la Paloma
  12 Oct: Discovery of America
  1 Nov All Saints'
  9 Nov: Virgen de la Almundena
  6 Dec: Constitution Day
  8 Dec: Immaculate Conception
  25 Dec: Christmas Day.

Spanish National Tourist Offices Overseas
- UK: ✉ 57–58 St James's Street, London SW1A 1LD ☎ 020 7499 0901
- Canada: ✉ 2 Bloor Street West, 34th Floor, Toronto, Ontario, M4W 3EZ ☎ 416 961 31 31
- USA: ✉ 8383 Wilshire Blvd, Suite 960, Beverly Hills, Los Angeles, CA 90211 ☎ 1213 658 71 88/71 92 ✉ 666 5th Ave, New York, NY 10103 ☎ 212 265 88 22.

Student travellers
- Viajes TIVE organised by the Comunidad de Madrid, offers many student travel discounts, travel cards and insurance ✉ Calle Fernando el Católico 88 ☎ 91 543 02 08 🚇 Moncloa.

Time differences
- Spanish time is one hour ahead of GMT.

Toilets
- Public toilets barely exist, and hygiene in bars and smaller restaurants is not always exemplary, though paper is generally available. Sometimes the key is kept behind the bar.

Tourist Offices in Madrid
- For information about the city: Municipal Tourist Office ✉ Plaza Mayor 3 ☎ 91 366 54 77/588 16 36 🕐 Mon–Fri 10–8; Sat 10–2
- For information about the area surrounding Madrid: Regional Tourist Offices ✉ Puerta de Toledo, in the market ☎ 91 902 100 007 🕐 Mon–Fri 9–7; Sat 9:30–1:30 ✉ Calle Duque Medinaceli 2 ☎ 91 429 49 51 🕐 Mon–Fri 9–7; Sat 9–1
- Tourist information is also available at Barajas Airport and Chamartín Station.

Women or lone travellers
- Common-sense rules apply.
- Avoid poorly lit areas and parks after dark.
- Women, particularly blondes, may attract wolf-whistles.

PUBLIC TRANSPORT

How to use the metro
- Station entrances are indicated by name and symbol.
- Passes are available for one month's travel. These also entitle you to travel on buses.
- Metro services run from 6:30AM until 1:30AM.

How to use the bus
- Routes run daily from 6AM until midnight, about every 15 minutes. All night buses (midnight–6AM) start in the Plaza de la Cibeles, but are less regular (every 30 minutes midnight–3AM; every hour after that).

- Flag the bus if it does not look as if it's stopping.
- Pay the driver or stamp your pass in the machine by the driver's seat.
- To request a stop, press one of the hard-to-spot red buttons.

Maps
- Metro maps are theoretically available from the ticket counter.
- Travel maps can be bought at newspaper stands (*kioskos*).
- Metro platforms have detailed local street maps indicating which exit leads where.

Types of ticket
- For the metro: *sencillo* (single journey) tickets from the metro stations. *Metrobus* tickets can also be bought from newspaper stands and tobacconists, giving ten rides on both the metro and buses; a *bono mensual* (monthly pass) entitles you to travel on both the metro and buses, and is available over the counter, with a photograph and identification.

Taxis
- These are cheap enough to make a reasonable travel alternative, particularly if you are a group of four. There are taxi-ranks in key locations, but normally you will have to hail a taxi.
- There is a charge for boarding, and a charge for every km travelled at more than 20km per hour. A supplement is also levied after midnight, and on Sundays and public holidays. Journeys to the airport incur an airport supplement. For longer journeys a cross-zone supplement is payable.
- Take only taxis with a green light on top. Check that the driver has reset the taxi meter before you set off, particularly if you are at a taxi-rank or the airport.

MEDIA & COMMUNICATIONS

International newsagents
- Foreign newspapers are normally available from *kioskos* beginning at lunchtime on the day of publication, and at about twice the home price. The *kioskos* at the western end of ✉ Puerta del Sol 🕐 24 hours ✉ Puerta de Alcalá ✉ Plaza de la Cibeles are reliable, with a range of foreign magazines. FNAC ✉ Calle Preciados and the various VIPS stores which also stock a good selection of foreign press.

Mail
- Buy stamps from post offices (few and far between) or tobacconists, which are indicated by a yellow and green 'T' sign on the wall.
- Madrid's most central post office, Palacio de Communicaciones, a huge building with many counters and long queues ✉ Plaza Mayor de la Cibeles ☎ 91 521 65 00/91 🕐 Mon–Fri 8:30AM–9.30PM; Sat 9:30–9:30; Sun 8:30–2
- Post boxes are yellow with two slots, one marked 'Madrid' and the other for everywhere else (marked *Provincias y extranjero*).

Newspapers and magazines
- The most important daily papers are *El País* (left of centre); *El Mundo* (centre); *Diario 16* (centre) and *ABC* (right of centre). The sports paper *Marca* is Spain's best-selling newspaper on Mondays. Good weekly news magazines are *Tiempo* and *Epoca*, while *El Mundo's* city guide, *Metropoli*, is published every Friday and is the best available. There is also the weekly *Guía del Ocio* (Leisure Guide).
- *Lookout*, an English-language monthly, is directed at English-speaking residents in Spain.

Telephones

- Public telephones take 5ptas, 25ptas and 100ptas coins. There is a minimum charge for an inner-city call.
- Phone cards are available from newspaper stands; most phones do not yet accept credit cards.
- Most bars have telephones; if not a pay-phone, you are charged according to the number of units you use.
- Telefónica (the Spanish phone company) has a huge public call office. You queue up for a cabin number, then pay afterwards at the central counter ✉ Gran Via 30 🕐 Mon–Sat 9AM–midnight Other public phones are at the Palacio de Comunicaciones in ✉ Cibeles 🕐 Mon–Sat 8AM–midnight; Sun and public hols 8AM–10PM ✉ Paseo de Recoletos 🕐 Mon–Sat 9AM–midnight; Sun and public hols noon–midnight
- Cheap rate for calls is 10PM–8AM daily.
- To call Spain from the UK dial 0032 followed by 91 for Madrid and then the seven digit number. No number needs to be dropped either inside or outside of Madrid.

Television and Radio

- There are five free TV stations in Madrid: TVE 1 and TVE 2 (state-run), TeleMadrid (local), Antena 3 (populist, biased) and Tele 5 (Silvio Berlusconi). The pay channel Canal + is good for films, sport and quality documentaries: like TVE 2, it shows original version films. Better hotels offer a range of digital TV channels.
- There are four national radio stations. Some non-Spanish speaking films and programmes can be seen on TVE1 and 2 although these are generally shown late at night.

EMERGENCIES

Embassies and consulates

Australian Embassy ☎ 91 441 93 50
British Embassy ☎ 91 319 02 08
Canadian Embassy ☎ 91 431 43 00
German Embassy ☎ 91 319 91 00
French Embassy ☎ 91 523 19 45
Irish Embassy ☎ 91 436 40 93
Italian Embassy
   ☎ 91 577 65 38/577 65 29
United States Embassy ☎ 91 577 40 00.

Emergency telephone numbers

Police (Local) ☎ 092
Police (National) ☎ 091
Police (Guardia Civil) ☎ 062
Ambulance ☎ 91 335 45 45
Red Cross Ambulance ☎ 91 522 22 22
English Language Helpline
   ☎ 91 559 13 93
Telephone Information (Spain)
   ☎ 1003
Telephone Information
   (International) ☎ 025.

Lost property

- Municipal Lost Property Office ✉ Plaza Legazpi 7 ☎ 91 588 43 46/44 🚇 Metro Legazpi 🕐 Mon–Fri 9–2
- For objects lost on a bus: EMT ✉ Calle Alcántara 26 ☎ 91 406 88 00 🚇 Metro Lista. Ask for *objetos perdidos.*
- For objects lost on non-metro trains, call the relevant station and ask for *objetos perdidos.*
- Report a lost passport to your Embassy.
- To claim insurance on a loss, notify a *comisaría* or police station.

Medicines

- Chemists (*farmacias*) are indicated by a flashing green cross; they are usually open 9:30–2 and 5–8. Outside these hours, all pharmacies post a list of *farmacias de guardia* (all-night chemists) and highlights the closest ones. There is also a list in the daily papers.

- Madrid's chemists are often quite happy to let you have prescription medicines without a prescription.

Sensible precautions

- Carry valuables in a belt, pouch or similar – not in a pocket.
- Do not wear bags over one shoulder.
- Do not keep valuables in the front section of your rucksack. If possible, wear your rucksack on your front on public transport.
- Be aware of street tricks around tourist attractions. These include distracting you in conversation, or spraying foam on your back and then offering to clean it off while someone else grabs your bag.
- Avoid parks at night. The *barrio popular* (south of the Puerta del Sol) has a high crime rate.
- Try to look as though you know where you are going.

LANGUAGE

- The level of English does not generally exceed 'OK'. Explain clearly, repeatedly and with hand signals. Spanish is phonetic, so once you master a few basic rules, you should be understood.

Pronunciation

c before an *e* or an *i*, and *z* are like *th* in thin
c in other cases is like *c* in cat
g before an *e* or an *i*, and *j* are a guttural sound which does not exist in English – rather like the *ch* in loch
g in other cases is like *g* in get
h is normally silent
ll is similar to *y*
y is like the *i* in onion

- Use the formal third person 'usted' when speaking to stranger; the informal 'tu' when speaking to friends or younger people.

Courtesies

good morning buenos días
good afternoon/evening buenos tardes
good night buenas noches
hello (informal) hola
goodbye (informal) hasta luego/hasta pronto
hello (answering the phone) ¿Diga?
goodbye adios
please por favor
thank you gracias
you're welcome de nada
how are you? (formal) ¿como está?
how are you? (informal) ¿que tal?
I'm fine estoy bien
I'm sorry lo siento
excuse me (in a bar) oiga
excuse me (in a crowd) lo siento

Basic vocabulary

yes/no sí/no
I do not understand no entiendo
I am not from here no soy de aquí
left/right izquierda/derecha
entrance/exit entrada/salida
open/closed abierto/cerrado
good/bad bueno/malo
big/small grande/pequeño
with/without con/sin
more/less más/menos
near/far cerca/lejos
hot/cold caliente/frío
early/late temprano/tarde
here/there aquí/allí
now/later ahora/más tarde
today/tomorrow hoy/mañana
yesterday ayer
how much is it? ¿cuánto es?
when? ¿cuándo?
where is the...? ¿dónde está...?
do you have...? ¿tiene...?
I'd like..... me gustaría
I don't speak Spanish no hablo español
I'm in a hurry tengo prisa
Where can I buy...? ¿dónde puedo comprar...?

INDEX

CityPack
Madrid

Written by Jonathan Holland

Edited, designed and produced by
 AA Publishing

Maps © The Automobile Association 1997
Fold-out map © RV Reise- und Verkehrsverlag Munich · Stuttgart
 © Cartography: GeoData

Distributed in the United Kingdom by AA Publishing, Norfolk House, Priestley Road, Basingstoke, Hampshire, RG24 9NY.

The contents of this publication are believed correct at the time of printing. Nevertheless, the publishers cannot be held responsible for any errors or omissions or for changes in the details given in this guide or for the consequences of any reliance on the information provided by the same. Assessments of attractions, hotels, restaurants and so forth are based upon the author's own personal experience and, therefore, descriptions given in this guide necessarily contain an element of subjective opinion which may not reflect the publishers' opinion or dictate a reader's own experiences on another occasion.
We have tried to ensure accuracy in this guide, but things do change and we would be grateful if readers would advise us of any inaccuracies they may encounter.

© The Automobile Association 2000
First published 1997
Reprinted Jan, Jun and Dec 1998
Reprinted Mar and Jul 1999

A CIP catalogue record for this book is available from the British Library.

ISBN 0 7495 2351 4

Published by AA Publishing (a trading name of Automobile Association Developments Limited, whose registered office is Norfolk House, Priestley Road, Basingstoke, Hampshire RG24 9NY. Registered number 1878835).

Colour separation by Daylight Colour Art Pte Ltd, Singapore
Printed and bound by Dai Nippon Printing Co (Hong Kong) Ltd.

Acknowledgements
The Automobile Association wishes to thank the following libraries and museums for their assistance in the preparation of this book: Bridgeman Art Library, London 37b. *King Henry VIII* by Hans Holbein the Younger, Thyssen-Bornemisza; 41 *The Naked Maja* by Francisco de Goya y Lucientes, The Prado; 47a. *The Adoration of the Magi* by El Greco, Museo Lazaro Galdiano. Mary Evans Picture Library 12. Museo Cerralbo, Madrid 27. Museo de America, Madrid 26b. Spectrum Colour Library 8, 52.
The remaining photographs are held in the Association's own library (AA Photo Library) and were taken by Rick Strange with the exception of pages 7, 29, 36, 38a, 43a, 43b, 50, 51 which were taken by Jerry Edmanson; pages 20, 21 taken by Philip Enticknap and pages 18, 55, 58 taken by Tony Oliver.

Cover photographs
Main picture: Spectrum Colour Library. Inset top: Pictures Colour Library.
Inset bottom: AA Photo Library (R. Strange)

MANAGING EDITOR *Hilary Weston*

Titles in the CityPack series
• Amsterdam • Atlanta • Bangkok • Barcelona • Beijing • Berlin • Boston •
• Brussels & Bruges • Chicago • Dublin • Florence • Hong Kong • Istanbul •
• Lisbon • London • Los Angeles • Madrid • Miami • Montréal • Moscow •
• Munich • New York • Paris • Prague • Rome • San Francisco • Seattle •
• Shanghai • Singapore • Sydney • Tokyo • Toronto • Venice • Vienna •
• Washington•